Science, Technology and the International Political Economy

Series Editor: John de la Mothe

The upheavals of the international political economy during recent decades have fundamentally altered the relationships between firms and states, citizenship and management, social institutions and economic growth. The changing pace of competition, firm performance and geo-economics is shifting the pressures on public policy and corporate strategy alike. As a result, our conceptual frameworks for analyzing key events, emerging trends and driving forces are being challenged. As unclear as the future is, what remains certain is that science, technology and innovation will occupy a central place. By looking at a wide array of issues – ranging from security and foreign affairs, the environment, international institutions, corporate strategy and regional development to research policy, innovation gaps, intellectual property, ethics and law – this series will critically examine how science and technology are shaping the emerging international political economy.

Published titles in the series:
Evolutionary Economics and the New International Political Economy, edited by John de la Mothe and Gilles Paquet

Systems of Innovation, edited by Charles Edquist

Universities and the Global Knowledge Economy, edited by Henry Etzkowitz and Loet Leydesdorff

Forthcoming titles in the series:
Innovation and the Service-Based Economy, edited by Ian Miles and Mark Boden

Innovation Strategies in Middle Power Countries, edited by John de la Mothe and Gilles Paquet

Regional Innovation, Knowledge and Global Change, edited by Zoltan Acs

Science and Technology and Governance, edited by John de la Mothe

Proposals for books can be sent directly to the series editor:
  John de la Mothe
  Program of Research on International Management and Economy (PRIME)
  Faculty of Administration
  University of Ottawa
  275 Nicholas Street
  Ottawa, Canada K1N 6N5

Global Change and Intellectual Property Agencies

An Institutional Perspective

G. Bruce Doern

PINTER

London and New York

Science, Technology and the International Political Economy Series
Series Editor: John de la Mothe

Pinter
A Cassell imprint
Wellington House, 125 Strand, London WC2R 0BB
370 Lexington Avenue, New York, N10017-6550

First published in 1999
© G. Bruce Doern 1999

British Library Cataloguing-in-Publication Data
A catalogue record for this book is available from the British Library.

ISBN 1-85567-532-3

Library of Congress Cataloging-in-Publication Data
Doern, G. Bruce.
    Global change and intellectual property agencies : an
institutional perspective / G. Bruce Doern.
        p.   cm.— (Science, technology, and the international
political economy series)
    Includes bibliographical references and index.
    ISBN 1–85567–532–3 (hardcover)
    1. Intellectual property.   I. Title.   II. Series.
K1401.D64 1998
346.04'8—dc21   98–26010
                                                                                                    CIP

Typeset by York House Typographic Ltd, London
Printed and bound in Great Britain by The Cromwell Press Ltd, Trowbridge

Contents

Preface

My research as a political scientist and author in public policy and public administration has concentrated in the last decade on different aspects of industrial policy institutions and regulation in a globalised economy. This research has included work on trade, R&D policy, competition, environment and the changing nature of regulatory regimes. Work in each of these areas always rubbed shoulders with the intellectual property system but the latter was an area that was not central to my interests. In this respect my attitude was very similar to the governments I was studying.

When my interest began to focus increasingly on this area of regulation and governance I looked first for basic published work that would give me a reasonable and basic *institutional* overview of intellectual property agencies and regulatory regimes. This book turns out to be the book that I could not find.

Research for this book has been a genuine voyage of discovery over the past three years. There was good and varied work to draw on from legal scholars and there was, of course, a vast and overwhelming array of technical literature and government and agency reports on individual agencies. There was a burgeoning literature, largely by economists but also lawyers on the trade-related aspects of intellectual property. In my own discipline, there was literature on the interest group politics of sectors such as the pharmaceutical industry and patents, but remarkably little on the agencies of intellectual property. There was no basic mapping of the array of institutions that came even close to dealing with the structure and interplay among national and international agencies and institutions, let alone the underlying cluster of political interests and interest groups in the IP field.

This book is an effort partially to fill this gap by providing a basic institutional perspective. The seven national and international intellectual property agencies are examined in a very basic manner and in the context of a broader changing industrial-trade-innovation policy agenda and a general effort to reinvent government towards better service delivery.

The analysis is based first on the literature cited and on related agency documents and reports. It is based secondarily on over 70 interviews carried out with officials in the seven agencies in 1996 and 1997. The discussion of the role of business, the IP profession and other interests is crucial but my sources here are secondary. A simple lack of resources did not allow me to carry out a complementary set of interviews with such stakeholder interests in all of the agency jurisdictions.

I am indebted to John de la Mothe for helpful comments on an earlier draft. Doug Kuntze and Lisa Power at the Canadian Intellectual Property Office were especially supportive in getting this work started and in nurturing it along the way with timely advice and encouragement. I also wish to thank the many people in the seven agencies and in other national ministries who kindly gave me their time and insights and some of whom have commented on earlier drafts of this book or on particular chapters. Hopefully, they will see some value-added from the views of an observer who tried to see their world in their terms but who also offers an applied institutional perspective on an increasingly vital set of economic players in national and international economic governance. The above people have certainly made this a better product but they bear no responsibility for any remaining errors or weaknesses in the analysis. These are my responsibility alone.

Special thanks are also due to several institutions which provided research funding and support along the way, including the Social Sciences and Humanities Research Council of Canada, the School of Public Administration at Carleton University, the Politics Department at the University of Exeter and the Canadian Intellectual Property Office.

G. Bruce Doern
May 1998

CHAPTER ONE

Global Change and the Core IP Trade-off: An Introduction

There is little doubt that intellectual property (IP) is commanding more attention as an issue than at any time in recent political economic history. Both the protection and the dissemination aspects of the core IP trade-off are a part of this new prominence. For many, IP is a crucial element for prosperity in a knowledge economy. For others, it is a kind of perverse new protectionism and a US-led effort at the globalisation of property, a substitute, in effect, for other earlier or declining forms of trade protection such as the tariff and industrial subsidies. At yet another level it becomes understood in even a populist context as a needed form of protection. Princess Diana is killed and the official charity created in the wake of her death needs to establish trademark and even copyright protection from bogus charities or other kinds of more exploitative enterprise. Even more broadly, the emergence of the Internet suggests to some that intellectual property rights will be virtually unenforceable and will establish a greater community ownership or free ownership of information and ideas. IP issues raise vital economic, social and moral issues in the patenting of life forms, and in matters regarding biodiversity.

The ultimate context for, and cause of, this rise in the importance of IP is global change in general (de la Mothe and Paquet, 1996; Bellamy and Taylor, 1998; Weiss, 1998). The key features of such change are well-known but are also bewilderingly complex and interdependent:

- the globalisation of production and the massive increases in the mobility of capital;
- the digitalisation of computer and telecommunications which escalate the formation of information and service-based economies and societies;
- the demise of the Soviet Union and the transformation of Eastern Europe;
- the entrenchment of free trade and the formation of competing trading blocs as well as competing countries;
- the obvious interdependence of environmental eco-systems in a shrinking world;
- the reinvention of government as the state is both caught up in change and seeks to influence and guide it in less bureaucratic and more innovative and democratic ways.

These compelling global changes also alter the nature of public policy formation and indeed transform the boundaries and focal points of policy fields and their political and economic constituencies. Science and technology policies writ large shift from a once simpler and even exclusive focus on R&D spending to a concern for whether a country is adept at establishing and using IP rights (Wallerstein,

Mogee and Schoen, 1993; Jasanoff, 1998). New technologies in materials, bio-technology, computer software and other fields are produced through varied and complex inter-firm and business–university alliances and partnerships. Innovation policies and actions are seen as more crucial than earlier forms of industrial policy, although the latter have not totally disappeared. More and more policies are cast as trade policies or as trade-related policies and hence realms of policy-making power inside and outside the state change (Doern, Pal and Tomlin, 1996). Trade policy hegemony is also seen as being driven by the global economic power of the USA but it also raises new problems in the relations between the developed and developing world (Hoekman and Kostecki, 1995).

Despite the explicit and implicit new status of intellectual property rights in the changing political and economic sun, intellectual property institutions are not well-known. IP agencies are, in fact, among the oldest national and international governmental institutions but they are among the least studied. Intellectual property and its main constituent parts – patents, trademarks, copyright, and designs – have been examined in great detail by legal scholars and economists and in specialist technical fora but a broad look at IP agencies as institutions has been missing (Jacob and Alexander, 1993; Bainbridge, 1994; Cornish, 1996). This is especially the case for those who are seeking to understand for the first time the basic institutional contours of the field. It is also a gap in the economics literature where the recent focus on trade and intellectual property has raised institutional issues but has still not provided a basic look at IP institutions as governmental regulatory and operational entities (Maskus, 1995; Baldwin, 1997).

The analysis of IP in the author's home discipline of political science and public administration has been at best tangential, not only on policy but even more with respect to institutions. Political analysis tends to focus on particular interest group sectors in patent policy such as the chemicals industry, pharmaceuticals, and bio-technology (Acharya, 1992; Greenwood and Konit, 1992; Ashford, 1996). These are important perspectives but the intellectual property policy and institutional arena itself is still treated in these analyses at best as contextual and secondary.

In the study of most policy and institutional realms such as social, industrial, trade or health policy, basic institutional examinations are readily available. This is not the case for intellectual property in the sense in which a political and administrative scholar would normally understand it.

Purpose and focus

The overall purpose of this book, therefore, is to provide an institutional examination of the nature of, and relationships among, four national and three international IP agencies. The four national agencies are:

- US Patent and Trademark Office (USPTO);
- UK Patent Office;
- Canadian Intellectual Property Office (CIPO);
- Australian Industrial Property Organization (AIPO).

The three international IP bodies are:

- World Intellectual Property Organization;

- European Patent Office (EPO);
- World Trade Organization (WTO).

The analytical focus is on institutions and the issues involved in the study and practice of international versus national bodies and the cooperative and competing relationships they have with each other in the globalised economy. The book is best seen as focusing on a middle level of institutional analysis for reasons which are set out later. The author essentially brings a relatively standard mix of analytical concepts and issues that have for the most part been derived from examining policy and regulatory institutions at the national level but which must also deal with how international institutions function.

These national-international institutional focal points are detailed later but one caveat about this approach must be made especially clear. Any examination of institutions must be set in a context of policy issues and debates but the need for a middle-level focus on operating IP institutions also means that policy issues are secondary in the overall scope and structure of the book.

If this were a book that was focused on IP *policy*, a different structure of analysis would be needed and it would have to deal much more thoroughly than this book does with crucial policy debates on the interplay between IP policy and trade, the Internet, competition, health care, and environmental policy (Bhat, 1996; Chartrand, 1996; Gallini and Trebilcock, 1996; Anderman, 1998). Some attention to institutions would undoubtedly be a part of such an alternative policy-focused book but institutions would be secondary, simply to be able properly to examine the array of policy concerns. It is also the case that the IP institutions that would emerge in a policy-focused study would be different, requiring for example, more of a look at each of industry, foreign policy, telecommunications, health and environment policy departments of governments and their clusters of interests.

This book tries to keep the focus on the four national and three international entities as regulatory and operational bodies that reside at the centre of IP institutions but around which many of the global changes are occurring. For the most part this means that we also have to set analytical priorities on the four main areas of IP as an operational system of protecting and disseminating intellectual property. Thus, throughout the book we look first and foremost at patents, then at trademarks, and then at copyright. We do not examine the issue of designs. Trade secrets are a further aspect of intellectual property that does not receive attention.

These choices and rankings are driven in part by the mandates, cultures and politics of the seven agencies. In most of the agencies, patents and trademarks are central to the mandates but with the greater prestige and power residing in and around the patent registration process. This prominence is partly a result of the fact that patents are examined through a process that involves scientific and technical judgement and competence whereas trademarks involve judgement that is closer to an art than a technical judgement. As we will see, there are also inherent differences in the regulatory 'rhythms' or cycles of patents versus trademarks and in their respective business constituencies and policy and service delivery communities.

Copyright aspects are in one sense only a third priority concern in our institutional focus. This is because the national 'patent' or 'IP' offices do not usually have a primary copyright mandate. Copyright institutions are different as will be made clear, partly because they typically do not centre on a registration process. But in another sense, copyright aspects assume a far higher priority concern in two respects. First, two of the international agencies (WIPO and the WTO) are concerned with copyright and second, copyright issues and politics are arguably the main driving force in international IP politics and hence are crucial to understanding how and why the set of IP agencies has changed in the 1990s.

All of this means that the book devotes more analytical attention to the patent aspects of the agencies and that trademarks and copyright receive second-order emphasis. But all three elements must be covered to some reasonable extent if we are to understand IP institutions in a basic way.

The nature of this mix of IP areas and their distribution across the seven agencies means that the book eschews a form of 'head-to-head' comparison either among the four national agencies or among all seven national and international bodies. The nature of comparison is more general in nature and this type of approach is deemed all the more necessary because of our interest in the changing relationships between national and international IP bodies and institutions. Thus, there is no single chapter devoted entirely to WIPO, EPO or the USPTO but rather the several agencies are discussed in several of the chapters. This is especially the case in those chapters devoted to understanding the inherently different activities and interests centred around the protection versus dissemination trade-offs in regulating IP.

The other obvious question regarding the comparative nature of the enterprise is the rationale for the choice of agencies. The choice of the international agencies is straightforward. WIPO, the EPO and the WTO are simply the main international IP operational bodies. The European Trademark Agency in Alicante is not examined largely because it has only recently been established (Office For Harmonization in the Internal Market, 1995). This is also true of the WTO but the need to examine the WTO to some extent is compelling because it is so obviously part of the macro politics of institutional change and of WIPO–WTO relations.

The choice of the four national agencies is essentially based on a mixture of reasons regarding analytical focus and practicality and finite research resources. All four have Anglo-American roots and relatively common and established agencies and IP legal cultures. A broader comparison of agencies (e.g. Japan, Germany) would undoubtedly have had analytical advantages in drawing out broader institutional differences. Again, this is why the book is cast as a middle-level institutional analysis. Some selective reference to other countries and their legal and related IP cultures is brought out but it is more contextual. These broader comparative references include those between countries such as France and the USA in the examination of copyright institutions in Chapter 7 and between developed and developing countries in the IP institutional debate as a whole.

However, the choice of the USA, UK, Canada and Australia makes sense given that a key part of the institutional focus centres on how national IP offices have been affected by pressures to reinvent government and by the more concrete exposure to the choices that this has opened up, or at least exposed, between the core functions of protecting versus disseminating IP. These pressures have arguably been most explicit in the Anglo-North American political-institutional context but the choice of country agencies also makes sense in another way as well. This is because the book deals with the way IP agencies are competing with, and feel threatened by, larger international IP agencies. I am interested in how smaller IP agencies such as those of Australia and Canada (the latter in the ambit of the North American dominance of the USPTO) are coping with such institutional realities. But I am also interested in how larger IP agencies such as the UK see their links with the EPO.

These and other institutional issues can be usefully drawn out from this choice of countries but it must be reiterated that a wider basis of comparison would undoubtedly also be of interest, depending on the analytical focus. As always, practical considerations are also crucial, not only research costs, language barriers and capacities, but also the simple practical need to keep the book to a manageable scope and size in a very complex IP institutional and policy world.

Because the book has been written to provide a basic look at IP agencies, its institutional focus is set out in two main steps. Following a brief discussion of definitions, the first element of an institutional focus is examined, namely, an introduction to the basic nature of the protection versus dissemination trade-off that drives the nature and regulatory culture of IP agencies and around which exists two broader clusters of interests. The chapter then examines the nature of middle-level institutional analysis, a level that centres on selected aspects of the growing interdependence between international and national agencies in the IP field.

The main components of IP

Intellectual property is often divided into two fields: 'industrial property' and 'copyright'. Industrial property includes protection by means of patents, trademarks and industrial designs. Copyright gives authors and other creators of works of the mind such as literature, music and art, rights to authorise or prohibit, for a certain period of time, certain uses made of their works. So-called neighbouring rights also supply rights to performers such as singers and musicians.

Stated somewhat more specifically, the four elements of intellectual property can in general be defined as follows (in any jurisdiction, however, detailed definitional reference must be made to the particular provisions of the law and practice):

- A *patent* is a monopoly right 'granted for inventions relating to new technologies. An invention can be a product, manufacture or composition of matter, an apparatus, a method or process or an improvement on any of these' (Baldwin, 1997, p. 51). The monopoly right provides inventors 'with the right to exclude others from making, using or selling their invention for 20 years from the date of filing a patent application' (Baldwin, 1997, p. 51).
- A *trademark* is 'a word, a symbol, a design, or a combination of these, used to distinguish the wares or services of one person or organization from those of others in the marketplace' (CIPO, 1994, p. 5).
- A *copyright* is a right to prevent copying of literary, artistic, and musical works. It arises automatically without a period of waiting for registration but does not give a complete monopoly in the way that patents do (Bainbridge, 1994). A copyright does not protect the underlying ideas or concepts themselves but rather protects the way an author or artist expresses an idea or concept. Other rights exist that are related to or 'neighbouring on' copyright and typically include: the rights of performing artists, the producers of phonograms, and broadcasting organisations (WIPO, 1995, p. 165).

- A *design* right is a means of 'protection for designs for industrial products' (Jacob and Alexander, 1993, p. 15). In some countries an unregistered design right arises, like a copyright, without any need for application or registration and it does not give a complete monopoly. More typically, however, a design must be registered. In essence, a design protects the appearance of articles but not the way they work.

Each of these basic broad working definitions also inherently begs the question of whether there is, in practice, a functioning intellectual property policy field as opposed to separate realms of patent, trademark, copyright and design policy, each marching to the beat of different political-economic drummers. To some extent, as will be seen, they are separate fields because of the different characteristics, situations, interests and traditions in each area. But there is no doubt that political, technological and economic pressure is also causing governments to fashion policy for the IP field as a whole, particularly given that modern economies are said to be knowledge driven.

Another basic way to see IP as a field is to appreciate how it has evolved at the international level. Three stages of overall development are usually portrayed (Merges, 1990; Marlin, 1995; Drahos, 1997). The first stage is a territorial or national stage where there were no international rules or regimes. Beginning in the latter part of the nineteenth century, an international regime emerges centred on the Paris and Berne conventions. It is still territorially based but extends the rights of creators through treaties. The most recent stage and the one which elevates it to its present state of political-economic centrality begins in the mid-1980s, with US-led pressure to globalise intellectual property. Various aspects of these stages are covered in later chapters, but first, we need to focus on the basic nature of IP institutions.

IP institutions I: IP protection and dissemination and basic clusters of interests

As operating institutions, IP agencies fundamentally exist to give practical expression to the central IP policy trade-off. In an overall sense this means regulating and administering a trade-off between protecting creations and inventions of the mind and disseminating such creations for the broader good of society. When looked at within a nation state, economists express the need for the state to determine such trade-offs because of the presence of a public good. Thus, in the first instance, the new intellectual creation is a public good because one person's consumption of it does not diminish anyone else's capacity to consume it (Maskus, 1995). Private markets could not easily prevent such consumption. Moreover, because such private actors could not appropriate the gains for themselves, they would have only limited incentives to innovate or create. Society would be worse off because secrecy would be encouraged and there would be an undersupply of such ideas, creations and innovations. This creates the case for state intervention but it does not in itself make the case for how far to intervene or what instruments to use to intervene (Patel, 1993; Trebilcock and Howse, 1995).

If, at the other extreme, the state intervenes and gives intellectual property creators and owners full control, then it is creating monopoly economic power, with resultant higher prices, economic inefficiencies in general, and a lessened exchange and use of the innovations themselves. Hence, there emerges the search for a regulatory or interventionist balance, in short a set of trade-offs between two principles or policy rationales that are both seen to be, in this sense, 'in the public interest'.

Another less economics-oriented way of expressing the policy choice inherent in IP is simply to ask who contributes to any given invention or creation and how much of it is individual, corporate or collectively and/or socially derived. Consider for stark comparative purposes an area far removed from IP. Those who study criminology engage in endless but always important debate and theory regarding the extent to which crime is caused by the individual compared to other economic and social contributing factors. Similarly, in the polar opposite spectrum of behaviour, acts of creativity, one can certainly see arguments about who shares in the process of creativity and who therefore ought to share the benefits. Inevitably, there is an individual, corporate and society-based mix of claims.

Within nations that have advanced IP policies, the tendency has been to characterise such policies as being 'framework oriented' in that the pressure is to define one overall trade-off rather than create special ones for different industrial sectors such as computers or pharmaceuticals. But in theory and in practice such varied sectoral trade-offs are also possible (Trebilcock and Howse, 1995; Park and Ginarte, 1997; Thurow, 1997).

When the core IP policy trade-offs are conceived among nations it follows that country-to-country differences in policy and IP institutional evolution could be justified depending upon whether a country's policy makers saw it as a country that was directly an 'innovating' one or was a country engaged largely in 'imitation'. Thus, in theory, there is 'nothing suspect or unreasonable with the preference of many developing countries for a relatively lax system of intellectual property rights' (Trebilcock and Howse, 1995, p. 251). For example, Japan practised such an imitation strategy with great success in the immediate post-World War II decades (Okimoto, 1989). So did the USA in the nineteenth century. Developing countries could gain considerably in terms of consumer welfare and hence a battle has long been present over what the optimum global policy might be (Frischtak, 1995).

Clearly, such trade-offs in an international context are not the product of some set of benign processes of economic calculation or inevitability. The political interests of nation states or regional trade blocs, and political institutions and interests within countries, both help determine where and how the trade-off will be made and how it will be continuously adapted.

There is little doubt that IP rights and the nature of the core trade-offs have moved to a higher plane on the international global economic and regulatory trade agenda. Many developing countries have devised IP policies that have provided quite short periods of patent protection (Siebeck, 1990; Frischtak, 1995). Developed countries such as Canada for some time also had such a policy regarding pharmaceutical drugs (Campbell and Pal, 1994). In recent trade debates and negotiations, the USA and, somewhat more belatedly, the European Union, have led the fight for both more stringent IP policies and policy enforcement. Concern about lax enforcement to deal with pirated products such as videos and recordings is a major concern.

All of this political pressure was also fuelled by a general recognition that the knowledge-based economy of the modern era was a different kind of economy from the past in that now intellectual property rights were especially crucial but not unambiguously so (Renko, 1987; Maskus, 1995). Thus both ideas about fairness and views of global versus national or regional economic welfare are at the centre of the international and national expression of the IP policy trade-off. Such trade-offs must, however, be made through a complex set of national and international agencies and institutions which are, in turn, pressured by business interests, the IP professions, various users of IP, and national governments.

The protection role is central to the existence of the seven intellectual property agencies examined in this book. They exist to establish rights to intellectual property. The protection role centres on five issues or processes:

1   the quality and efficiency of pendency performance or of the central processes of granting patents and registering trademarks, particularly, given the focus of this book, the patent examination process;
2   issues and debates regarding the length and quality of patent protection and IP protection in general;
3   national and international enforcement and compliance issues, especially in the context of copyright;
4   the role of big business in giving focus to the protection function;
5   the role of the IP professions (patent lawyers and agents and trademark agents) as intermediary interests between IP applicants and the IP agencies but whose primary interest is also in the protection function.

The IP dissemination role as a whole is both an old and new role for these same IP institutions. The oldest IP dissemination role is that of making available to IP users in the economy the current information held in the stock of patents, nationally and globally. A second more recent variation on this role arises when IP bodies and national industry departments see opportunities, through computer information technologies, to make available to business new value-added kinds of commercially useful information from IP information held by the government. A third kind of IP dissemination arises in the form of efforts to expand awareness of IP among those parts of a national or regional economy and society which have not yet sought IP rights so that more firms will use the IP systems and contribute to a more innovative economy. In some instances, such efforts can be seen as campaigns to produce an IP culture in a country that may be lacking one.

The IP dissemination roles as a whole attract a different and much more dispersed array of interests than does the protection role in that small and medium-sized businesses, individual inventors, universities, R&D organisations and fast-forming knowledge networks and consulting firms are involved. This does not mean that big business and the IP profession have no stake in these roles. They are also major users of IP information. Rather, what happens is that a wider set of interests inherently coalesce around these roles. The roles are more diffuse than the protection role and so are the interests.

IP institutions II: changing relations between national and international IP agencies

If the first aspect of our conceptual portrait of IP institutions is about a fairly basic notion centred around protection and dissemination and related clusters of interests, the second aspect is more complex and layered in its component parts. To introduce it we look at four elements:

- the nature of institutional approaches;
- IP agencies as national agencies and bureaucracies within national governments;
- IP agencies as international bureaucracies;
- key features of the evolving relationships between IP national and international agencies.

The nature of institutional approaches

This book does not seek to focus on any kind of elaborate discussion of the vast literature on the study of institutions, bureaucracies and complex organisations. It employs an institutional perspective but its larger purpose is to provide an initial useful middle-level way of understanding IP agencies. Nonetheless, it is important to see briefly how institutions have been viewed conceptually since we seek to derive insights about the IP agencies from several of the strands of institutional analysis.

A governing institution can be thought of as an entrenched set of values or rules and hence it is structured by the external and internal constraints of the organisation or body involved, including its culture of operation (March and Olsen, 1989; Ostrom, 1990). But institutions are also historical constructs. Early formative choices have a pervasive influence over later decisions. Regulatory bodies such as an IP agency can and do change but not without overcoming these internal features which may be seen as valued features by some interests and inertia by others (Weaver and Rockman, 1993; March and Olsen, 1989). Even more structuralist conceptualisations of government institutions exist which highlight more fundamental veto points or constraints on how subsets of public policy or institutional change are made or are allowed to be made (Searing, 1991; March, 1996).

Institutional analysis by economists has tended to focus on institutions as aggregates of individual preferences and hence the reform of regulators and regulations is seen to turn on either getting rid of unproductive rules or redesigning them with the appropriate new mix of incentives that will produce more efficient outcomes (Ogus, 1994). A more holistic notion of institutions as prior or larger sets of beliefs or views of the public interest tends to be eschewed and indeed is a suspect concept among mainstream economists. There are, however, more recent strands of institutional analysis by economists that are broader and more in line with how political scientists and many practitioners have always seen governing institutions (North, 1990; Yarbrough and Yarbrough, 1990; de la Mothe and Paquet, 1996). In short, they focus on a more historical evolutionary form of economics, analyse systems of trust and cooperation, and seek to locate the core structure of individual incentives in larger sets of complex relationships (Levy and Spiller, 1996).

In the broadest sense, these evolving approaches to the study of institutions have mainly been applied to, and based on the study of domestic or national governing, policy and regulatory institutions or bodies. The study of international institutions, however, has been far less likely to have been examined with this kind of mix of approaches with a middle-level focus on operating agencies in mind. This is because the study of international institutions has been largely the preserve of international relations scholars whose primary analytical focus has been on foreign policy, international political economy and relationships of power among nation states (Elkins, 1995; Bennett, 1995; Pollack, 1996). Indeed, international institutions are only a smaller subset of this academic discipline and international agencies *per se* are rarely the focal point of study in a focused concerted way. This may be due, in part, to the inherently greater practical problems of access in penetrating the international institution compared to many national governing bodies in various fields.

As Taylor and Groom observed in the late 1980s, 'the academic study of International Relations has been characterised by the use of the state as the basic unit of analysis and the dominant school of thought ... has been the power or "realist" school' (Taylor and Groom, 1988, p. 4). They observed further that the 'study of international organization and institutions is in a serious imbalance' (Taylor and Groom, 1988, p. 5). By this they meant that institutions and regimes at a basic macro level were a concern in international relations study but not agencies at a functioning level as organisations.

In recent years this has begun to change. First, globalisation and a world with fewer borders have compelled scholars of international relations and domestic or national public policy to enter each other's analytical worlds (Doern, Pal and Tomlin, 1996). A useful example of this is Susan Sell's analysis of the recent development of intellectual property policy and institutions at a macro world level in comparison with competition or antitrust policy development (Sell, 1995). She builds on developments in international relations theory which extend the realism school into a more subtle mixture of neo-realism and neo-interpretivist subschools. The former still centres on power and coercion and the latter focuses on the role of learning and sources of change. Her analysis shows that the former provides a better explanation of what happened to US-led intellectual property changes at the global level whereas a neo-interpretivist approach was more persuasive for understanding the looser forms of antitrust development. This example shows a kind of extension of focus by scholars in international relations within the state and its policy fields but it is still at a macro level.

A second impetus for change at the international relations level is the burgeoning study of the European Union (EU). The EU has almost by definition compelled more analysis of national and international (EU) bodies as interacting regimes of governance, policy making and implementation (Richardson, 1995; Majone, 1996). No obvious or dominant model of such a new nexus of national and international institutional analysis has emerged to date and indeed the literature is often confined to the level of useful case studies (Pollack, 1996; Kreher and Meny, 1997).

The present book also necessarily exhibits some of this middle-level and agency case study approach as it seeks to supply an initial institutional examination of several IP agencies whose worlds are increasingly changing in ways that make them simultaneously cooperating and competing bureaucracies.

IP agencies as regulatory agencies within national governments

As regulatory bodies within national governments, IP agencies need to be examined with several institutional elements fully in mind as derived from regulatory and other literature (Majone, 1996; Doern and Wilks, 1998). In the book as a whole, we look at several such elements:

- the core rhythms of activity and organisational culture central to the basic regulatory existence of the agencies, i.e. their production cycle surrounding applications for patents and trademarks;
- the larger mix of functions that any such body carries out, such as related service and advisory roles;
- the financing of the organisation;
- the political saliency of the organisation and its policy field within its ministry and the government as a whole;
- its relationship to 1990s government-wide reforms, particularly those centred on the reinvention of government and the so-called new public management, the latter propelled by political-managerial theory and ideology but also by the communications revolution centred on the Internet (Campbell, 1996; Ferlie, *et al.*, 1996; Aucoin, 1997).

A central feature of these governmental and managerial reforms has been to make governmental agencies more conscious of their diverse customers and users and to be more entrepreneurial towards meeting their needs (Ferlie, *et al.*, 1996).

With regard to each element in this list, I am interested in how it constitutes a reasonably accurate picture of the 'internal' organisation as such, but I also seek to extend these features outwards to some extent to see how they are affecting its main interests, or stakeholders. It must quickly be added, however, that the analysis of external interests in this book is a general one, focused on the cluster of interests sketched out earlier rather than on a detailed analysis of particular business, professional, and other lobby and stakeholder groups that surround each agency in each country or jurisdiction.

IP agencies as international bureaucracies

In looking at IP agencies as international bureaucracies and institutions, our analytical attention is initially on several of the same features: core production cycles and cultures; the mix of functions; financing and the like. But key attributes of international bureaucracy then need to be folded in and drawn attention to. These include:

- organisational membership centred on national governments;
- the tendency for slower-moving consensual decision making; issues of language and related legal cultures;
- the fact that private interests (business, NGOs) have more indirect access (through their national governments) to agencies compared to the access they have in national agencies;
- the slower and more difficult penetration of the reinventing government ethos in international institutions.

National-international agency relations and issues

Not surprisingly, the interaction between these national and international institutional features produces a mixture of IP institutional relationships and issues, some of which can be seen clearly and others of which can only be explored in a more speculative context. In this complex web of changing relations, we focus on four key changes and issues of importance:

1   the greater exposure of the tension inherent in the IP trade-off caused by the combined effects of global change, US hegemony in the IP agenda, and the pressure to reinvent government;
2   the continuing dominance of the protection role in the core technical cultures of the main IP agencies;
3   the financial interdependence of national and international IP offices and its links to the conflict over the future role of national versus international IP offices as nations seek to promote so-called innovation cultures or IP cultures;
4   the issue of second-tier protection (such as petty patents) or even more democratised IP as several interacting forces and interests combine including the needs of small and medium-sized business and the onslaught of the Internet.

The greater exposure of the tension inherent in the IP trade-off arises from the fact that political-institutional developments are forcing some of the issues more into the political limelight. On the one hand, the US-led trade agenda seeks to globalise the protection of property to a considerable extent. On the other hand, more subdued but quite real changes involving reinvented government are pressing the agencies to see their roles more broadly, which means essentially to draw out their dissemination roles more significantly.

But the upper hand is still undoubtedly found in the protection function and its links to the twin interest clusters that support it and are nourished by it: big business and the IP profession. The protection function is central to the culture of the IP agencies and to its production and technical case-handling roles.

The third issue to be examined in the nexus of relations between national and international bodies centres on genuine dilemmas about which institutions will play, and pay for, the broader IP dissemination functions and exactly how these fit in in an era where innovation policies are more the norm, supplanting previous industrial policies dominated by the tariff and the use of subsidies. Agency finances and capacities and the roles of broader industry departments are a part of this puzzle.

Finally, and more speculatively, recent developments raise issues about the existence of second tiers of IP protection and about the democratisation of IP institutions writ large arising from the growth of the Internet and from a reaction against the recent era of the globalisation of intellectual property.

Structure and organisation

Through a focus on the interplay of these middle-level national-international institutional dynamics and issues, the book examines IP institutions as governmental regulatory agencies interacting with clusters of interests.

Chapter 2 is essentially descriptive and supplies an initial look at the basic nature of their core application and operational cycle focused first on the patent field. The chapter also sets out the core mandates of the seven agencies, many already reconfigured in the 1990s to conform with the ethos of reinvented government.

Chapter 3 focuses on the institutional development of the 1990s including how IP agencies are seen within national governments in relation to longer term industrial policies and more recent efforts to cast industrial policy as innovation policy.

Our attention then shifts to a closer look at the way interests align around the two functional aspects of the IP trade-off, especially in the realm of patents. Chapter 4 focuses on IP protection and the key interests which coalesce around it, especially big business and the IP professions.

Chapter 5 then concentrates on the IP dissemination functions and the much more dispersed sets of user interests that revolve around them.

In Chapters 6 and 7 we look at some of the different institutional dynamics in the related trademark and copyright fields of IP. As already mentioned these areas are a secondary focus in the book but cannot simply be ignored if the agencies as institutions – national and international – are to be understood.

Chapter 8 then examines the growing influence of the World Trade Organization under the provisions of the TRIPS agreement. These changes have begun to affect significantly the relationships between WIPO and the WTO and are crucially the result of pressures from American IP institutions and business interests. Finally, in Chapter 9 conclusions are offered, centred around a discussion of the key institutional aspects introduced earlier.

National and International IP Institutions: The Core Patent Cycle of Business and Basic Mandates

The analysis begins in a basic descriptive manner. In this chapter we take a brief initial look at the core application cycle for patents and at the basic mandates of four national IP agencies of the USA, the UK, Canada and Australia and two of the main international bodies, the World Intellectual Property Organization (WIPO) and the European Patent Office (EPO). In each case, the basic mandates of the agencies are described. There is also brief reference to related IP institutional developments centred on the WTO and put in place in the wake of the Uruguay Round Agreement on Trade-Related Aspects of Intellectual Property (TRIPs). The WTO will be examined more completely in Chapter 8. Subsequent chapters will add successive layers of flesh to this initial bare bones description.

While important variations emerge among the mandates described, these brief portraits must essentially be seen first in the context of not only the policy trade-offs already sketched out in Chapter 1, but also in terms of the basic internal case or application decision cycle and stages for patents. This is first described in a stylised fashion so as to appreciate the central business of IP agencies. The cycle for trademarks is examined in Chapter 6. Copyright decision processes are different largely because in most countries there is no application/registration process and thus for this, and other reasons, copyright will be dealt with in Chapter 7.

The central business of IP institutions: the application cycle for patents

The exact cycles for patent applications vary across national and international agencies depending upon legal requirements, regulatory philosophies (e.g. first to invent as in the USA versus first to file) and language and other constraints, but an overall cycle can be presented for patents. In the description that follows, the Canadian system is set out for illustrative purposes but the real intent is to show the essence of the business IP agencies are in – in short, their dominant or basic rhythm of activity particularly concerning the patent protection role.

Tens of thousands of patent applications traverse the core IP agencies and by its very nature, this volume of business establishes the key features of the organisational culture of the agency. It is very much a technical activity where examiners in the IP office with technical expertise in various core disciplines in engineering and science assess applications, interacting with technically expert and legally expert players on the side of the inventor or applicant. As in many regulatory bodies, the rhythm of cases and the sequence of steps drive the organisation on a day-to-day, month-to-month basis.

Two other features of these core organisational realities are noteworthy. The first is that every national IP agency needs a basic minimum core capacity of examiners for it to function properly. Conventional wisdom suggests that at least 100 examiners are needed to cover the basic technical disciplines. This is not a problem for major countries but it can be problematical for countries whose agencies suffer a reduction in volume of patent business and whose national offices' future existence may then be threatened or called into question by competition from international bodies.

The second additional feature to note is that, until the 1990s, the typical IP agency was not in the least in the political limelight and hence the case rhythms and cycles were even more the driving feature of the IP regulatory culture. It was a routine 'business as usual' world.

Under Canada's Patent Act, patents are given to the first inventor to file an application. The information given to potential patent applicants suggests a multi-step sequential process. If an individual inventor calls the Patent Office, he or she is advised to find a qualified patent agent. If the patent agent is in a larger law firm, the individual first-time inventor applicant typically meets with a junior, technically qualified lawyer or a patent agent *per se* who goes over the invention with the applicant/inventor. A search for prior patents and other publications is then done by the lawyer or agent.

To be patented an invention must demonstrate novelty, utility, and inventive ingenuity; hence a preliminary search, if it finds a relevant patent, or other disclosure, may simply end the process right then and there. But if the invention is deemed to be new, the crucial task of the patent lawyer or agent begins.

The task of preparing a patent application is a process which essentially involves writing a description of the invention and writing claims which 'draw a fence' around the invention in order to define it, so as to distinguish it in a patentable sense from other existing patents and other disclosures. Inevitably, this is a process that involves discussion between the inventor and the patent lawyer or agent but it also draws on the agent's own technical knowledge and experience, including patent law and practice requirements.

An application is then formally filed at the Patent Office consisting of a written petition, description of the invention and claims, and a fee. At this stage, no patent is guaranteed. At this point, too, the inventor knows that in 18 months a notice will be published in a Patent Office Record indicating the application and hence information in it will be available to others. An application is not automatically examined. Examination must be formally requested. If not requested within a 5-year period after filing, the application is considered abandoned.

The examination process, once requested, can take two to three years to complete. The application is classified at filing according to the International Patent Classification (IPC) system. It then goes to one of the patent examiners who are themselves broadly grouped in scientific/technical disciplines or groups consisting of mechanical, chemical and electrical technologies. Their examination of the file involves a search of existing patents and related technologies and information sources, and examination of the application for statutory compliance.

There then follows a prosecution stage when something akin to bargaining and negotiation can occur arising out of different professional judgements between the patent examiner on behalf of the public interest and the patent agent on behalf of the applicant. Some claims in the patent application may have to be redrawn because, in the examiner's view, they define technology which is known to the public and do not meet the tests of novelty, utility, and ingenuity. In effect, these discussions/ negotiations are precisely the point at which the boundary is drawn between the inventor's legitimate rights and the public interest, i.e. protection is provided in return for sharing the technological information with the public. The patent agent tends, within limits, to press for the maximum protection of the patent fence on behalf of the applicant. The Patent Office examiner must protect the rights of the public but at the same time grant the applicant adequate rights in conformity with the law and to ensure that new ideas are not unduly hampered.

During this examination phase, the applicant must meet or overcome each objection raised by the examiner. There may also occur at this stage discussions between the patent agent and the inventor about whether it is wise, economical or prudent to continue. This is the expensive part of the application process in that the patent lawyer or agent's fee clock is ticking. Hence, there emerge the often classic debates about whether the costs of the process are too great. Inventors, or at least the small inventor, may at times feel that he or she is being 'strung out' by a procedural conspiracy among lawyers, patent agents, and examiners, all lumped into one category of villain, known simply as 'the system'. Alternatively, patent agents and lawyers see this stage, and the process as a whole, as involving a small cost for the inventor to pay relative to:

- the future gains to the inventor from a valid patent;
- the losses avoided by not proceeding with an invention that is not patentable or which results in later infringement suits.

If the patent application is accepted, then the inventor pays a further fee to the patent office. Annual maintenance fees must also be paid both during pendency and after the patent is issued.

Ultimate enforcement of patent rights is done through private rights enforcement which involves law suits against persons who infringe patents. The patent office does not have a patent police force, although its examination process is itself a form of scrutiny of the scope of protection granted to individual patents. The full patent cycle also contains a process whereby a granted patent may be reexamined at the request of either the patentee or a third party.

By the same token, if the patent application is rejected, a review process is available. The review process is not itself established by statute. Instead, in the Canadian example used here, a Patent Appeal Board, made up of senior Patent Office officials, considers the arguments set forth by the patent examiner and corresponding agent's response and advises the Commissioner of Patents. The Commissioner then issues a decision since it is the Commissioner as a statutory person who grants or denies a patent. The Commissioner's negative decision can be appealed to the Federal Court of Canada and, ultimately, to the Supreme Court of Canada.

There is one further important aspect of the overall patent application process. The description just given was for a single national office but patent processes can also involve processes facilitated by the Patent Cooperation Treaty (PCT). Prior to its coming into force in 1978, the traditional patent system required the filing of individual patent applications for each country for which patent protection was being sought. This was both expensive and time consuming.

The PCT does not enable the granting of an international patent since the responsibility for granting patents remains a national responsibility (World Intellectual Property Office, 1995, Chapter 20). But it does establish a system which enables the filing with a patent office (the receiving office) of a single application (the international application) in one language having effect in each of the countries party to the PCT (89 contracting states) which the applicant designates in its application. The receiving office provides a formal examination and the application is forwarded to one of nine PCT international search authorities (ISAs) which conducts an international search and develops a report citing the relevant prior art which should be taken into account in deciding whether the invention is patentable. The report is made available to the applicant first and it is published later. The PCT system also provides for centralised international publication of international applications and the reports mentioned earlier. It also provides the option of an international preliminary examination.

The application process then shifts to the national phase. The remaining granting procedure is the task of the designated office, i.e. the national office of, or acting for, the countries which have been designated in the international application. This designated office could also be an international regional authority such as the European Patent Office.

The PCT process also involves only a single set of fees for the preparation and filing of the international application which are payable in one currency and at one office. National fees are payable later.

IP agency mandates in brief: going beyond the protection function

IP agency mandates and roles at the national and international levels essentially revolve around the central rhythms of the IP business. But the patent cycle and the trademark cycle (see Chapter 7) are basically those of the regulatory or IP protection role and hence we have yet to capture, descriptively or analytically, other features of the institutional business of IP agencies, in short, their broader range of functions, such as their IP dissemination, service and policy advisory roles. The profile of agency mandates that follows allows us to move further in this direction but still in a descriptive mode. The profiles essentially cover their mandates or missions and some key features of their basic structures.

The US Patent and Trademark Office

It is instructive first to note that US IP institutions are rooted, in effect, in the United States Constitution. Article I, section 8 asserts the goal central to the creation of intellectual endeavour, namely 'to promote the progress of science and the useful arts by securing for limited times to authors and inventors the exclusive right to their respective writings and discoveries' (US Patent and Trademark Office, 1995, p. 5). The USPTO's origins as an office can be traced to 1802 when a separate official in the Department of State was placed in charge of patents. A formal office, the USPTO was established in 1836 and by 1925 it had moved to the Department of Commerce where it resides today as one of the department's fourteen bureaux. At present a non-commercial federal entity, the USPTO's 5000 employees administer its major functions, namely the examination and issuance of patents and the examination and registration of trademarks.

A 1995 review document describes the patent and trademark mission as that of promoting 'industrial and technological progress in the United States' and strengthening the national economy by:

- 'administering the laws relating to patents and trademarks;
- advising the Secretary of Commerce, the President of the United States, and the Administration on patent, trademark, and copyright protection;
- advising the Secretary of Commerce, the President of the United States, and the Administration on the trade-related aspects of intellectual property' (US Patent and Trademark Office, 1995, p. 1).

Thus, the USPTO is not the main administrator of copyright law (see Chapter 8) but is involved in related policy matters on copyright and on IP as a whole.

The head of the USPTO is an Assistant Secretary of Commerce who is also the Commissioner of Patents and Trademarks. As head of the office, the Commissioner exercises general supervision over the USPTO and also prescribes the rules, subject to the approval of the Secretary of Commerce for such matters as the conduct of proceedings within the USPTO and the recognition of attorneys and agents.

As Chapter 3 shows, proposals are being actively pursued to make the USPTO into a semi-independent government-owned corporation. Since 1990, however, the USPTO has evolved into a quasi-business-oriented agency. Propelled by the new service ethos in public management circles and by the requirements of the US Government Performance and Results Act of 1993, the USPTO was reorganised in 1994 and committed itself to numerous actions for meeting customer needs. The old organisational structure was replaced with a 'process and customer based' structure (US Patent and Trademark Office, 1995, p. 12). Customer service activities were given a concerted focus through employee training, enhanced timeliness of service targets and enhanced telecommunications computer-based service delivery.

There is little doubt that the USPTO is, along with Japan's IP agency, the hub of the world patent system in terms of absolute volume. In 1994 US patent applications exceeded 200,000 and patents issued exceeded 113,000 (US Patent and Trademark Office, 1995, p. 8). Like other IP offices, US concerns centred on reducing the 'pendency rate'. Increasingly, the USPTO faced an increased volume of business and a commercial environment in which 'the rapid advancement and innovation of technology today requires a patent protection system that is swift and adaptable to the needs of individual inventors, small businesses, and multinational corporations' (US Patent and Trademark Office, 1995, p. 8).

The UK Patent Office

The main aim of the UK Patent Office is 'to stimulate the growth and development of those areas of commerce and industry based on new ideas and technologies, through the establishment of industrial property rights ... and to help literature and the arts flourish through an effective copyright law' (UK Patent Office, 1990, p. 3). The objectives of the Patent Office are:

- to ensure that the intellectual property system operates in a way which reflects the national interest;
- to provide all its customers with services which combine quality with value for money;
- to ensure that industrial policy rights under its authority carry with them a good presumption of validity in the marketplace;
- to maintain the considerable knowledge and experience accumulated in the course of its work and to ensure these are available for the benefit of industry and commerce;
- to promote an awareness of the value of idustrial property and its exploration;
- to ensure that it performs its functions with increasing effectiveness, efficiency and economy (UK Patent Office, 1990, p. 3).

The UK Patent Office became an executive agency in 1990 with additional financial independence added in 1991 when it was granted trading fund status. The agency has a staff of just over 1000 persons, 93 percent of whom are based in Newport, South Wales, a move from London carried out in the midst of its becoming an executive agency.

The agency's framework document is careful in stressing that the Chief Executive is first, by statute, the Comptroller General, an independent statutory person. Among the Chief Executive's required functions are those of paying heed to 'the wider objectives of the Department of Trade and Industry (DTI)', including 'ensuring that when representing the UK in international fora, the interests of all users of the intellectual property system are fully taken into account'.

It was originally the Chief Engineer and Scientist, as Deputy Director for the Patent Office, who was stated to be the 'principal link between the Patent Office and the rest of the department'. But with regard to accountability to ministers, it is the Chief Executive who reports 'to DTI ministers on the work of the Agency'. Currently, it is an assistant secretary of DTI, with the assistance of a steering board, who is responsible for advising ministers on the adoption of the corporate plan (which includes Patent Office proposals on the setting of financial and other targets, and examination of major policy issues, including major investment decisions). The agency's framework also states that policy on the price of services, in other words on the key determinant of the Patent Office's income, are put to ministers and also require Parliamentary approval.

On operational matters, the Patent Office documents show that it has been subject to, and has achieved all its 1990–95 performance targets, a factor which, along with meeting other service standards, contributed to the agency being awarded one of the first Charter Mark Awards in 1993 under the UK Citizen's Charter initiative (UK Patent Office, 1994, p. 39). The agency has also been involved in the UK's 'market testing' programme which has resulted in several of its activities being contracted out rather than carried out internally.

Last, but not least, in this initial description of the UK Patent Agency, is the nature of activities given emphasis in recent annual reports. One concerns the agency's policy directorate, a function which still resides in London. The policy directorate has been heavily engaged in establishing and harmonising domestic and international policy and is actively involved with the World Intellectual Property Organization, the European Patent Office, and the European Union. The other concerns the growing emphasis on marketing and information dissemination. The latter includes a series of roadshow campaigns 'promoting awareness of intellectual property' and thus shows a desire to complement or rebalance the agency trade-off roles between protecting intellectual property and enhancing its use.

The Canadian Intellectual Property Office (CIPO)

CIPO's mandate is to 'accelerate Canada's economic development by encouraging the utilization of the IP system and the exploitation of IP information' (CIPO, 1994, p. i). Its operations entail the 'establishment of principles, policies, and procedures that enable clients to obtain intellectual property protection'. It also sees its basic capacity as being one which 'requires the accumulation of an extensive and diverse information base upon which utility, ingenuity, and originality can be judged' (CIPO, 1993, p. 3). Furthermore, it requires 'assembling and maintaining the expertise to make these judgements, ensuring there is a basis upon which decisions can be made, and disputes resolved, in a fair and equitable manner' (CIPO, 1993, p. 3).

CIPO is the focal point for the regulation and management of Canada's intellectual property system. Associated now with Industry Canada but formerly, until 1993, a part of the Department of Consumer and Corporate Affairs, CIPO is a Special Operating Agency (SOA), financed by a revolving fund, and hence has special management powers and financial flexibility designed to make it a better and more service-conscious organisation.

CIPO's mandate deals with patents and trademarks as well as with other realms of intellectual property such as copyright, industrial designs, and integrated circuit topographies. CIPO itself must be differentiated from the role of the Commissioner of Patents and Registrar of TradeMarks. The Chief Executive Officer (CEO) of CIPO is also the Commissioner and the Registrar. In the latter capacities he or she is a statutory person whereas in the role as CEO, which is the Industry Canada administrative title, he or she is an ordinary senior public servant. The role as a statutory person is important because most of the regulatory powers reside in this legally defined role.

This means that the Commissioner has an independent regulatory role vis-à-vis the Minister of Industry and the Deputy Minister of Industry Canada. This is to ensure that decisions on patents and trademarks are based on independent objective judgements and not on political considerations. In other respects, however, as CEO of CIPO, he or she is within the jurisdiction of the minister and department in the normal way. For example, if legislative policy changes were being considered to the

Patent Act they would be the responsibility of the Minister advised by his department, and by CIPO. CIPO at present reports to the Assistant Deputy Minister (ADM) for Operations but has policy links with the ADM for Policy as well. The CEO of CIPO is also responsible to his Minister and to the Treasury Board for functioning properly within the contractual obligations established for its status as a Special Operating Agency and financial operations on a revolving fund. With the revolving fund, CIPO accesses its own revenue earnings, which eliminates its dependence on general budgetary appropriations.

CIPO's business plan stresses many of the intertwined and converging developments facing IP agencies. Its SOA 'Charter' from the Treasury Board defines its mandate as the acceleration of Canada's economic development by:

- fostering the utilisation of intellectual property systems and the exploitation of intellectual property information;
- encouraging invention, innovation and creativity in Canada;
- administering the intellectual property systems in Canada;
- promoting Canada's international intellectual property interests (CIPO, 1993, p. 4).

The CIPO Business Plan goes on to stress that its SOA status is designed to facilitate an exchange of 'flexibility in return for performance' and that this means above all 'the achievement of continuous improvement in the quality and in the delivery of CIPO service' (CIPO, 1993, p. 9). Accordingly, CIPO has been reorganised to give new emphasis to its clients and to its product lines. CIPO is not funded through tax dollars but rather through client fees, 70 percent of which is earned from offshore, with 90 percent of the latter coming from patents.

CIPO sees its clients, in order of listing as: 'current and future creators of intellectual property; the employers of intellectual property – the innovators who capitalize on its economic potential; and agents that facilitate acquisition of intellectual property rights' (CIPO, 1993, p. 10).

The Australian Industrial Property Organization (AIPO)

AIPO's overall mission is 'to provide industrial property rights which enhance innovation, competitiveness and trade for the benefit of Australia' (AIPO, 1994, p. 1). It is a 730-person agency based primarily in Canberra. Like the Canadian IP agency, it represents a consolidated version of the previously separate Patent Office, Trade Marks Office, and Designs Office. It has evolved out of legislation first passed between 1903 and 1906.

AIPO is formally a part of the Department of Industry, Science and Technology but also has 'an identity under the statutes, separate and distinct from the Department' (AIPO, 1994a, p. 1). Hence, AIPO emphasises that it has a large degree of operational and financial independence, a status considerably enhanced by its move in 1993 to a Group 2 Trust Account under the Australian government financial system. It is now required by government policy that AIPO recover its full costs from charges for its services.

Like the other IP agencies surveyed in this chapter, AIPO has undergone several reviews and internal discussions aimed at clarifying its mission, commercialising its operations, and identifying its clients. Its strategy documents are much more explicit than those of the countries surveyed in precisely identifying its clientele. AIPO states that it is 'required to balance the interests of a broad range of groups, the most significant of which are: creators; users; the Australian Government; the Australian Public; overseas trade interests; international industrial property organizations; staff; and co-facilitators' (AIPO, 1994, p. 8).

Its vision for the next decade is expressed in terms of how AIPO would like to be viewed by each of these key 'relationship groups'. In brief, AIPO would like to be recognised as 'a highly visible, dynamic organization' which is:

- facilitating the growth of industry and commerce;
- fostering innovation and competitiveness;
- contributing to the provision of an effective trading environment for Australia;
- a highly rewarding workplace;
- a leading industrial property organisation (AIPO, 1994, p. 8).

Thus AIPO is seeking to modernise itself in keeping with new commercial realities and visions of a reinvented public administrative delivery system. AIPO also inevitably has particular priorities and features emerging from its own regional political economy, such as a concerted focus on the Asia Pacific region (AIPO, 1994, p. 22).

The World Intellectual Property Organization (WIPO)

Headquartered in Geneva, WIPO is one of sixteen specialised agencies of the United Nations system of organisations. There are 151 member states of WIPO, with another seven states being party to treaties administered by WIPO but not yet members. WIPO itself was established by the 'Convention Establishing the World Intellectual Property Organization' signed at Stockholm on July 14, 1967, which came into force in 1970.

WIPO's lineage, however, is more than a century old in that its functions can be traced to the 1883 Paris Convention for the Protection of Industrial Property and the 1886 Berne Convention for the Protection of Literary and Artistic Works. Both conventions provided for secretariats which eventually became, under various names, one international bureau. At the centre of WIPO's tasks were the various 'Unions' with each union founded on a multilateral treaty (e.g. the Paris Union, the Berne Union) – fifteen unions in total each with different numbers of signatory states.

The objectives of WIPO are to:

1   promote the protection of intellectual property throughout the world through cooperation among states, and where appropriate, in collaboration with any other international organisation;
2   to ensure administrative cooperation among the intellectual property unions (WIPO, 1995, p. 7).

Divided into the two main branches of intellectual property, industrial property and copyright, the promotional objective is carried out in a variety of ways. These include WIPO's active encouragement of the development of new international treaties (and hence new unions) and the modernisation of national legislation. It also includes technical assistance to developing countries, the assembly and dissemination of information, and the provision of services for facilitating the obtaining of protection of inventions, marks and designs for which protection in several countries is desired.

With regard to the complex administrative cooperation among the unions, WIPO centralises the administration of the unions in the International Bureau in Geneva. This is an immensely detailed task carried out amid decision and review processes that involve different combinations of membership for each union.

WIPO's relationship to the United Nations is also important in understanding it as an institution. Under Article 1 of its Agreement with the United Nations, WIPO is responsible for taking appropriate action in accordance with its basic instrument and treaties 'for promoting creative intellectual activity and for facilitating the transfer of technology related to industrial property' to the 'developing countries in order to accelerate their economic, social and cultural development' (WIPO, 1995, p. 9).

As an organisation, WIPO has three governing bodies:

1   the General Assembly composed of countries which are members of WIPO and members of the Paris and/or Berne Unions. The General Assembly adopts the biennial budget of expenses common to the Unions;
2   the Conference composed of all countries which are members of WIPO. It adopts the biennial budget of the Conference;
3   the Coordination Committee composed of countries elected among the membership of WIPO and the Paris and Berne Unions. This committee meets in ordinary session once a year whereas the other two bodies meet every two years.

As the secretariat of WIPO, the International Bureau is headed by the Director General and has a staff of 474, including the nationals of 63 different countries. At present about 73 percent of the income for WIPO's operations (total income in 1995 approximately 120 million Swiss francs) come from fees paid by the private users of WIPO's international registration services, with 18 percent coming from contributions from member states and 9 percent from the sale of WIPO publications and incidental income (WIPO, 1995, p. 67).

Of the four international registration services that WIPO's International Bureau operates, the Patent Cooperation Treaty (PCT) Service is undoubtedly the most important, and by far the biggest source of income. Centred on the Patent Cooperation Treaty of 1970 a patent application may be filed, as we have described earlier, and that will secure entry into each of a number of countries specified either by filing with the member country of origin or with WIPO's International Bureau.

The European Patent Organization

The European Patent Organization is a regional international body of member European states established under the European Patent Convention (EPC) signed in Munich in October 1973. Currently composed of seventeen member states (but with others set to join) the European Patent Organization was established to foster a Europe-wide patent system. It is important to note that it is not an institution of the

European Union, but rather an independent organisation composed of two organs, the Administrative Council and European Patent Office (European Patent Office, 1992).

The Administrative Council is composed of delegates from the contracting states. It adopts the budget, amends regulations and rules related to fees and appoints the President and Vice President of the European Patent Office as well as chairmen of the boards of appeal.

The European Patent Office (EPO) is the executive-administrative arm which exists to grant European patents using a unitary and centralised procedure. Patent protection in all member states can be obtained by filing a single patent application in one of the three official languages (English, French or German). Although the EPO is not synonymous with the European Patent Organization, it is generally referred to here as if it were.

The objectives of the EPO are cast in terms of the stated advantages of the 'European patent system' for different players in the system. For applicants it offers: 'a cost-effective and time-saving way of applying for patent protection in several different countries', a 'strong patent' and 'easier enforcement of rights' (European Patent Office, 1995, p. 13). For the contracting states, the system offers a reduced duplication of work, cooperation on patent documentation and more effective patent law through harmonisation with the EPC. For other users, the system offers access to the latest technologies, the facilitation of technology transfer and information on technical and market trends.

The EPO's 3800 employees are centred in Munich and The Hague with suboffices in Berlin and Vienna. Its budget of over DEM 1 billion is paid for entirely from procedural fees and a proportion of renewal fees for patents. Spurred both by the efficiency of the regional system and by the growing integration of the European economic system in the 1980s, the use of the EPO has considerably exceeded initial expectations. When the EPO was opened in 1977 annual patent volumes were expected to rise to about 30,000 annually but by the early 1990s this figure had doubled.

It is evident, therefore, that the EPO's mandate deals only with patents. The development of a European trademark and designs system has only recently been given an institutional base. In this case, the institutions are centred in the European Union, namely in the Office for Harmonization in the Internal Market (OHIM) (Trade Marks and Designs). Located in Alicante, Spain, the OHIM began its community trademark functions only in 1995, and hence it is too soon to comment on its activities – only on the fact that it is established.

Unlike the EPO, the office is established under European Community law and is supervised by the Community courts. Like the EPO, it must derive all of its revenue from registration and renewal fees. An application for a Community trademark may be filed in one of the official languages of the European Union. However, any post-registration proceedings must be in one of the five languages of the Office (Spanish, German, English, French and Italian). A more restricted number of languages was deemed necessary to reduce operational burdens and the level of fees.

The WTO and TRIPs

The WIPO and EPO (and national offices as well) must increasingly be linked to the newer provisions in the trade agreement on 'trade-related intellectual property rights' or TRIPs and to the formation of the World Trade Organization (WTO). The WTO and TRIPs is examined in Chapter 8 but an initial sketch here is useful in the context of this chapter because these institutional connections are increasingly crucial.

Under the pre-Uruguay GATT framework, the international IP regime fell well short of a harmonised regime. Indeed, IP issues were largely outside the GATT purview, e.g. regarding Most Favoured Nation provisions and aspects of National Treatment principles. Moreover, WIPO did not contain a formal court-like process for dispute resolution. It regularly reported on disputes but had no GATT-like panel process for dispute resolution (Trebilcock and Howse, 1995).

The Uruguay Final Round Act includes for the first time a comprehensive agreement on TRIPs that seeks to balance the conflicting values inherent in IP and between developed and developing countries (Braga, 1995). It also establishes a new body, the Council on TRIPS which is examined in Chapter 8. As we will see, these changes had particular implications for WIPO whose political space was invaded by a powerful new institutional presence.

Conclusions

Our first look at the seven national and international IP agencies has necessarily been a largely descriptive one. The agencies essentially revolve around the core business or case application cycles for patents and trademarks. The case routines and volume essentially produce a technically centred organisational culture. A network of case-centred relationships develops among the agency's examiners, individual and business inventors and the IP professions. The application cycle for patents has been described in a stylised manner but is an essential starting point for institutional analysis. The trademark cycle is examined later in order to appreciate the important second line of business of most IP agencies.

The actual mandates and missions of the particular agencies have also been described and reveal some differences in emphasis, as well as broad similarities. Differences range from the partial constitutional status of US IP rights to the varying degrees to which the agencies have embraced the recent credo of commercially oriented, independent and client-oriented 'reinvented' agencies. Similarities arise in the kinds of emphasis given to the classic historic role of protector of IP rights but all the agencies are seen to be giving more overt recognition to the broader IP dissemination roles. This means a broadening sense of their own clients and of the interests with which they must develop close working relations.

Differences in governing structure emerge between national and international bodies but we need to know much more about both kinds of agencies before we can assess the nature of the relationships between national and international bodies, including changes that may arise out of the TRIPs agreement in the Uruguay Round.

CHAPTER THREE

The Evolution of Intellectual Property Agencies in the 1990s

The focus in this chapter is on two basic aspects of the lead IP organisations or agencies: their governing structure including relations with parent ministries or governing bodies; and the place of IP in the overall industrial/economic policy and priorities of the governments and jurisdictions involved. In this account there is further reference to financial and personnel issues and related aspects of organisational culture but a more detailed analysis of these features is best left to the discussion in Chapter 4 of the core IP protection role.

The focus is still on broad developments and basic trends in the 1990s rather than on further detailed descriptions of each jurisdiction's features. As both aspects of institutional evolution are examined, there is a necessary separation in the two sections of the chapter between the international bodies (WIPO, EPO and WTO) and the group of national IP bodies examined. The growing relationships between international and national IP bodies is the focal point of the book as a whole but, at a very fundamental level, as stressed in Chapter 1, there are important differences in the basic dynamics of governance of the international bodies compared to the national agencies.

Governing structures: emerging from contented obscurity

The basic features of IP agency mandates have been described in Chapter 2 and hence a starting point already exists for understanding IP governing structures. Arguably, the most important point of departure for the 1990s is that both international and national IP bodies are, in a real sense, for the first time being politically discovered and are being paid more continuous attention by their political masters. This is somewhat of a paradox in that, as we have seen in Chapter 2, the core patent agencies are among the oldest in government, internationally and within many countries. The core IP agencies were politically 'out of sight, out of mind' within national governments, in part because the field is very technical and even arcane for laypersons and because patent and IP policy was not seen as being central to the evolving and variously named industrial policies of most western countries (with Japan being an important exception) (Okimoto, 1989). The various national patent offices and WIPO were extremely operational in nature and hence functioned in contented obscurity. In the last decade, this state of affairs changed markedly and its impacts on basic IP governing structures can be seen at both the international and national levels.

International bodies

The governance of IP international bodies is best seen in two ways: the generic nature of international agencies; and the basic governance structures and dynamics of WIPO and the EPO.

The most basic fact about international agencies is that their governing structures are composed of signatory member national governments (Taylor and Groom, 1988; Taylor, 1993). The national representatives who sit on or attend the governing council or assembly meetings thus bring to the international body both an interest in the body and its success but also a concern for the strategic interests of their own country/government. They also bring the concerns of the home ministry or agency from which they come within a national government. This latter element is often not brought out sufficiently in more macro-oriented studies of international organisations and institutions.

The typically large membership of international bodies (albeit across a wide range of sizes) also makes their formal decision-making and governing processes slow and unwieldy. Decision making typically must secure a high degree of consensus. Frustration with these processes and/or the sheer need for action often requires the aggressive action of active coalitions among a smaller subset of member states or from a lead 'hegemonic' member state (Kratochwil and Mansfield, 1994; Bennett, 1995). The permanent secretariat of the agency is also a key influence either in slowing down development to reach a broad consensus or, occasionally, through its own leadership's active role (in effect, bureaucratic entrepreneurship and risk taking). The dynamics of the international agency are also affected by whether it has a one member one vote system or a weighted system of voting favouring the larger or more powerful countries.

In this section, we can only glimpse some of these features, but they can be first seen in the context of WIPO. WIPO is the first of the international agencies in that, even in its modern era, it predates the emergence of the EPO as a regional international body and certainly predates the mature functioning of the EPO which really takes shape only in the mid-1980s (Bogsch, 1992; World Intellectual Property Organization, 1995).

As Chapter 2 hinted, WIPO is a complex organisational mélange. It is a UN agency but has considerable independence largely because, in contrast to most UN agencies, it has its own independent source of funds (see more in Chapter 4). WIPO has a three-level governing structure (General Assembly, Conference, and Coordination Committee). It has upwards of 151 member states whose interests and priorities vary across the patent, trademark and copyright realms, and in relation to the priorities that ought to be accorded to its trio of basic functions:

- norm setting and advancing the development of IP standards across the world;
- administering the various 'unions' or IP conventions;
- cooperative activity, especially regarding the needs of developing countries.

Since there were and are varying memberships in the different unions, WIPO's meetings can have extremely complicated voting procedures. Its basic financial structure is also reflective of a considerable dispersal of power among member states in that, first, about 85 percent of its funding comes from fees from private sector patent applicants for the use of the registration system, especially via the Patent

Cooperation Treaty (PCT) (Bogsch, 1992). Of the small part of its money that comes from member states, no one state pays more than a very small share. This means that large countries such as the USA do not obtain a disproportionate influence out of the very structure of weighted voting and budget contributions, as is the case in other UN and international bodies (Taylor, 1993).

All of this suggests the image and reality of a slow moving international agency that must, in essence, inch its way along in an increasingly fast changing world. However, WIPO must also be seen, perhaps alone among the agencies surveyed in this book, in terms of the continuity of its leadership. From 1973 until his retirement in 1997, WIPO's Director General was Arpad Bogsch, an American international civil servant, whose personal imprimature on the organisation is part of its culture. A tenacious workaholic, Bogsch involved himself in virtually every detail of the organisation. Albeit in a very bureaucratic way, he ensured that it ran as a relatively efficient operational agency compared to any other UN agency. Bogsch, with a keen eye on its diverse membership, insisted that its broad overall mandate serve both the needs of the developed and developing world (Bogsch, 1992).

If tenacious but bureaucratic leadership and a complex governing structure produced an often sound operational agency, it also produced, especially in the 1990s, an increased frustration among key members with the capacity to change IP policy in the global economy, especially regarding enforcement issues in developing countries. In this context, the USA, but also the European Union countries dis-played increased impatience with WIPO and its slow consensus processes and agendas. The politics of copyright policies and laws, increasingly linked to trade negotiations and enforcement mechanisms, were a particular catalyst for change (Abbott, 1989; Curtis, 1990; Warshovsky, 1994). This is further discussed later and in Chapters 7 and 8, but in terms of the present focus on governing structures, the main point to stress is that WIPO's processes were undoubtedly, and understandably slow, and that it was, like most IP organisations, mainly an agency concerned with patent and trademark issues rather than with copyright because the former were at its operational core. As later chapters show, WIPO was also criticised from within and without in the Bogsch era as an agency that was too geared to narrow legal approaches and that was slow to adjust to the technological imperatives of the Internet.

By definition, the European Patent Office is undoubtedly a less complex inter-national body than WIPO. It has only seventeen member states and, as its name implies, it is concerned with patents only (European Patent Office, 1995). Without doubt, the key feature of the EPO's governing Administrative Council is that, in the main, the national representatives that sit on that council are the heads of national patent (IP) offices. The majority of these national offices in turn (see later) typically report in their own national governments to industry departments (the German Patent Office being a significant exception in that it reports to the Justice Ministry). The presence, in particular, of the heads of patent agencies from major countries with patent offices such as the UK, Germany, Switzerland and Sweden is especially important. Such representatives invariably bring a dual set of interests within the Administrative Council, that of their obligation to implement the European Patent Convention through the EPO, and that of their concern for their own national patent office, whose functions are partly threatened by the very existence of the EPO.

The dynamics of the EPO's council and operations are also affected by the fact that many member states do not have patent offices or operate more limited registry offices (e.g. France, Holland, Italy) or have much less developed cultures and interests in intellectual property such as the southern European states (Spain, Portugal). At the same time, many of the key states across these ranges of IP interest are extremely concerned about the language in which commerce is conducted (European Patent Office, 1994a; 1995). Hence, issues such as the translation of patents into major European languages are a key feature of both high politics and practical administrative fees, costs and delivery (see Chapter 4).

The operational independence of the EPO is reinforced by the fact that it meets all of its budgetary needs through its patent fees. The fact that it is not an agency of the European Union (EU) also gives it operational autonomy. But this may be changing for some of the same reasons we have seen already for changes in the politics of WIPO. In brief, other aspects of intellectual property policy are within the jurisdiction of the EU and its Commission in Brussels. As mentioned in Chapter 2, a European (EU) trademark agency has begun operations in Alicante, Spain (Office for Harmonization in the Internal Market, 1995). But, more important, copyright policy, and key aspects of patent policy in a larger European EU sense are a growing policy concern in Brussels. The Directorate Generals in the EU Commission, that deal with competition policy, industry, innovation and the internal market, are increasingly active in discovering the importance of IP writ large. In this emerging context, the EPO may or may not be 'in the loop' regarding policy matters. It is certainly not automatically consulted, but the EPO cannot help but be aware of some of the changes through the antennae of the national representatives from national patent offices.

The national offices

What trends in the governing structures of the four national offices as a whole are evident in the 1990s? Three trends seem to permeate the four-country sample and thus warrant discussion:

- the continuing importance of the 'statutory person' model of governance to prevent political interference in individual patent and trademark applications/ examinations;
- the move, under the ethos of reinvented government, to executive or special agency status within national governments (with new client and customer advisory mechanisms);
- the handling of the IP policy function between the IP agency and its parent industry department.

The statutory person model

Given the pattern of broader changes, it is easy to forget the continuing importance of the statutory person model of organisation. In the UK, Canada, and Australia, it is to one or more single statutory persons (rather than multi-person commissions) to whom the IP laws assign legal responsibility for the issuance of patents and the registration of trademarks. This is partly because Canadian and Australian systems were modelled on earlier British laws and institutions. But among the countries as a whole there has been an avoidance of the use of collective multi-member commissions as the mode of regulatory organisation.

The preference for the statutory person is rooted in a desire to ensure that patent decisions are arrived at on the basis of objective technical knowledge and consideration rather than 'small-p' or 'big-p' politics. This is all the more necessary in globalised markets if international firms and users of IP information are to trust the integrity of IP decisions on individual applications.

The USA also adheres to this model on a de facto basis even though the governance of the US Patent and Trademark Office (USPTO) is overlain with the system of political appointments (the so-called spoils system) in which the top layers of the US Administration change each time a new President is elected. Thus, the current Commissioner of Patent and Trademarks, Bruce A. Lehman, is also the Assistant Secretary of Commerce, a Clinton presidential appointee (US Patent and Trademark Office, 1994). So too are three other senior officers of the USPTO. In essence, the 'career' or civil service appointees begin one rung further down.

In the patent and trademark field this nominal politicisation has not created problems since there is also great value placed in US political and business circles on the integrity of their patents and trademarks. The only recent concerns raised in some quarters is the view that the current incumbent, Bruce A. Lehman, is a person with a copyright career background and that, as one of the Clinton Administration's key advisors on IP trade matters, he is more preoccupied with those issues than with the traditional operations of the USPTO. But in none of this perspective is there even the slightest suggestion that the USPTO has become more political at the day-to-day operational level.

The move to executive or special agency status

While the 'statutory person' model is a vital holdover from the past, without doubt the most important recent development in basic IP agency institutions is the adoption in all of the nations of new forms of independent 'reinvented' corporate governance. Whether cast as executive agencies or special operating agencies, the tendency has been to give the agencies a wider range of legal or de facto powers over their finances, personnel and other operations (Doern, 1994; Ferlie, *et al.*, 1996). These forms were intended to free the agencies from as many of the government-wide disciplines on finance and personnel as was feasible.

Stated more positively, as we saw in Chapter 2, the changes were intended to foster greater efficiency in resource use and management and to facilitate a cultural change so that the agencies would be more aware of, and sensitive to, the needs of its full range of clients and customers (United Kingdom Patent Office, 1990; Canadian Intellectual Property Office, 1993). Indeed, even regulatory and compliance activities were to be cast under this mode of reinvented government as 'services' to customers.

In general, the evidence from the four jurisdictions suggests that the degrees of freedom have been greater in financial realms than in those of personnel. The national offices are all virtually or totally 100 percent dependent on fee income with the larger portion coming from patent fees (examination/granting and maintenance or renewal fees). They are able to carry over funds from one year to the next and can invest in capital improvements. Perhaps the one financial freedom they are denied is the right to set their own fees. This is typically left in the hands of the various Treasury ministries and/or with the parent industry ministers where it is guardedly watched over because of the general sensitivity of fee changes in micro-industrial policy politics and because of the Treasury's concerns about 'user fee' policy across the government.

On the personnel side of the agency status question, progress is seen as more sluggish, and moreover, judgements of progress are inevitably bound up in the larger accompanying efforts to create a greater service ethos. These are best left for discussion in Chapters 4 and 5 but attention can be drawn to at least two reasons why the personnel-oriented aspects are slower moving. One is that public service union issues are involved.

The other is that the technical composition of the IP staff, and the extremely detailed work involved in the examination process is very inward-looking and even isolated in its basic nature. Thus, suddenly transforming an organisation into an outward and nimble customer-oriented agency is difficult, not because people are excessively resistant to change but because, if they change too much, the inner integrity of the IP examination can, in fact, be harmed.

Beyond the general largely positive preferences for reinvented agency status, there are important differences in degree among the national offices. Two differences in the UK and US cases are illustrative of differences in the recent political climate in each country.

In the UK context, the Patent Office became an executive agency in the context of a Conservative Government that was energetically devoted to transforming virtually the entire British Civil Service into such forms of organisation. But the process went even further. All such agencies are subject to periodic review to determine if they should remain agencies or should potentially even be privatised. The UK Patent Office was so appraised in 1994 with at least some voices arguing before the Minister of Trade and Industry that it should be privatised. Following a consultant's review, the Minister concluded in December, 1994, that it would remain as an executive agency. The point to stress about this UK situation is that actual privatisation was seriously considered and that the agency is still left under continuous pressure as to whether it will continue to exist, with further uncertainty for agency personnel.

The US debate about corporate status is also rooted in the peculiarities of the US Congressional system. The USPTO had for several years been adopting many of the features of a service-oriented reinvented government agency (US Patent and Trademark Office, 1995). But in recent years the specific idea of converting it into a government corporation status has been expressed concretely in competing Congressional and Administration bills. Spurred on by a general reform of government initiative led by Vice President Gore, in which the USPTO is seen already as an exemplar, the Congressional initiatives have also been joined by particular agendas regarding the USPTO.

Large US firms want an independent agency that could run more efficiently. Smaller inventor groups are suspicious of such moves and their voices are heard in Congressional offices. And the USPTO has used the opportunity to point out such questionable financial practices as the one which requires the USPTO to turn over about 10 percent of what it earns in fees to the US Congress which keeps parts of it for its own projects. To make matters more volatile, the debate about the USPTO's corporate form was also embroiled in efforts to abolish the Department of Commerce, the USPTO's parent department (about which more will be said later).

The policy function

In historical terms, national patent offices have been perceived to be basically operational entities rather than policy bodies because they focused on their routine examination functions. But their operational image also flowed from the fact that, over very long periods of time, patent or other IP policies did not change very much (Doern, 1987). In fact, like many areas of business framework law, it was hard to get politicians and governments interested in policy change: to put it crudely, there were few votes there. The issue of generic drugs and health care costs are an exception, perhaps, but in general there simply has not been a broader public that politicians could interest in the issue for very long. In the late 1980s and early 1990s, however, two changes drew attention to the policy function. First, as the next section will show, the more that IP policy was linked with trade policy, the more frequently IP policy began to change. Second, the establishment of the previously discussed executive agencies was premised in some governments on the theory that the executive agency would deal with operations while the parent department would deal with policy.

But with regard to the formal separation of policy and operations, the four-country sample in fact reveals some important differences in how the policy function was assigned as agency status was conferred.

In the case of Australia, the AIPO simply maintained its previous policy role in an apparently non-controversial fashion. The parent Department of Industry, Science and Technology (DIST) had little expertise in the patent and trademark areas and hence there was no battle over jurisdiction in a general sense. This ease of continuity may also have been due to the fact that there had been a tradition of frequent personnel exchanges between DIST and AIPO over the years. The one area where DIST claimed some primary policy jurisdiction was in the field of pharmaceuticals. Its pharmaceutical sector branch had always been aware of and knowledgeable about the place of IP in this industry and hence it asserted a policy role on IP matters as they affected this sector. Pharmaceuticals are thus an exception but, as IP literature shows, this is an industry that often drives IP agendas in most western countries (Eastmann, 1985; Feketekuty, 1991; Warshovsky, 1994).

The UK and Canadian decisions regarding the assignment of the policy function were somewhat different from the Australian case. In the case of the UK Patent Office, the result after negotiations was that the Patent Office kept its policy directorate and called it that. In the case of the Canadian Intellectual Property Office (CIPO), the policy function was placed in the Industry Canada domain. CIPO's Planning, International and Regulatory Affairs Branch conducts some policy studies but the policy work is closely related to CIPO's operational concerns and requirements.

For the UK Patent Office, the early negotiation and retention of the policy function was regarded by the agency as crucial. The issue was resolved in a direct discussion between the Permanent Secretary of the Department of Trade and Industry (DTI) and the Chief Executive of the Patent Office but with other players at the centre of DTI arguing that the policy function should belong to the department. The agency's view was that if DTI took the policy function, in short, the agency's ten or so persons doing policy work, DTI would quickly run it down to a one- or two-person shop simply because of the pressure of budget cuts. The agency believed that even if the policy function were taken from it, it would quickly have to reinvent it. The reason was a simple one. In the final analysis only the agency had the real expertise and it expected that, in any crisis, the minister would come to it anyway. In the end, the agency secured the policy directorate and kept it in London because this was where most of DTI's other overall policy people were located.

CIPO's policy development rests within Industry Canada and was not the subject of negotiation. Its policy roles go through a Director General in charge of corporate governance or business framework policy, who in turn reports to the Assistant Deputy Minister for Policy. This place in the hierarchy stands in contrast to the overall agency SOA-status reporting relationship which is a direct one with the ADM Operations of the Department and then to the Deputy Minister. But even within these relationships, other factors may prove more decisive, certainly expertise. It remains the case that the larger policy shop lacks technical expertise, except perhaps in the copyright realms.

Once again, the USPTO must be treated differently from the three UK modelled agencies in that policy functions in a Congressional system of government are shared. When IP laws are being changed the legislation is negotiated. As we have seen, there are about four political appointees in the USPTO hierarchy. In the past, these have produced periodic incursions from the Department of Commerce but vast realms of policy and operational independence were left to the USPTO. In the 1990s the perception of a strengthened policy presence from political sources is strong but a discussion of this must await the larger discussion that follows since it clearly encompasses copyright issues, the growing trade–IP policy nexus and hence is larger than agency versus parent department relationships.

The place of IP in industrial and economic policy priorities

In the first section of this chapter, the focus has been on the immediate realm of governance of the IP agency itself and of its basic links to parent departments or similar structures. However, this must now be tied into a larger array of changes that can be seen to arise from the changing place of intellectual property policy in the industrial and economic policies of the jurisdictions being studied. This is not a journey that can be easily summarised but a basic portrait of change is crucial. In this regard, we need to discuss four aspects of change, the main import of which is to show that IP policy is indeed now a much higher priority of the governments in question but that IP is not unambiguously separable from a host of features needed to ensure that a country has a vibrant innovating economy. The four aspects profiled are:

- the demise of so-called traditional industrial policy;
- the ascendancy of trade-related and driven competitiveness and innovation-oriented policies;

- the emergence of intellectual property policy as such in a larger conception of innovation;
- the role of copyright concerns within IP, linked explicitly to the aggressive leadership and power of the USA.

The demise of traditional industrial policy

For the purposes of this chapter, traditional industrial policy refers to a variety of policies practised by most western governments to advance in the national interest key sectors of their economies (Wade, 1990; Doern 1995a; Coates, 1996). Although they occurred in the 1950s to late 1970s amid an underlying trend towards liberalised international trade under successive GATT rounds, such industrial policies employed mixtures of traditional tariff protection as well as expenditure subsidies. If there were concerns about the overall innovativeness of the economy (and there were) they would tend to be expressed in terms of the adequacy of R&D expenditures and other aggregate measures of comparison. Patent policy and other aspects of intellectual property were a component but were several steps removed from the political and economic consciousness of policy makers and, with some sectoral exceptions, from business lobby groups as well.

Canadian, British, and Australian industrial policies certainly conformed to this overall pattern. The USA was sometimes portrayed as a non-practitioner of 'industrial policy' because, it was argued, it implied a level of state-directed activity and targeting that was illegitimate in Americans' political culture of populist capitalism. Such qualifications, however, belied the fact that the USA did in fact practice de facto industrial policy, much of it sheltered under the umbrella of defence policy.

This era and pattern of industrial policy declined gradually but, by the early to mid-1980s, its demise could be clearly seen. In part, the decline occurred because of the gradual emergence, multilaterally and regionally, of new rules or pressures to end subsidy practices. Because of budgetary deficits, governments also were simply running out of money and could not afford the subsidies. Governments with a much more ideological opposition to industrial policy and state intervention took power and began acting on those beliefs. For example, in the UK, Thatcherism redefined 'industrial policy' by essentially arguing that it was a delusion (Hogwood, 1984; Wilks, 1993). Some Thatcherite ministers advocated the abolition of the Department of Trade and Industry (DTI) and in the 1980s it suffered from 'decimated budgets, minimal prestige, demoralized staff, and a series of disastrous ministerial appointments which included eleven Secretaries of State over 13 years' (Wilks, 1993, p. 240).

In this period of demise, industrial policy was also being severely criticised by mainstream economists in the four countries. Such policies, it was argued, were not only not successful but also, economists maintained, large sums of money were being wasted because subsidisation was often justified on promises to adjust and adapt but that such adjustment rarely happened (Best, 1990; Doern, 1995a).

In the heyday of industrial policy and in this period of decline, IP issues would from time to time emerge, but never centre stage or even close to that status in the economic agendas of national governments. In a similar way, the international changes in IP such as the emergence of WIPO and the EPO in the 1970s took place in a manner which was scarcely noticeable to national microeconomic policy communities.

The ascendancy of trade-related competitiveness/innovation policies

From the early to mid-1980s on, the economic policy focus shifted towards, and was driven by, trade-competitiveness agendas and by trade ministries. Within national governments this meant that the policy focus may or may not have been led by traditional industry ministers. In the UK, the trade jurisdiction was with DTI whereas in Canada, Australia and the USA, jurisdiction on trade resided more with foreign policy and/or trade ministries, and frequently, at crucial times, with prime ministerial offices.

Crucial to understanding the entire period from 1985 to the present is that it has been characterised by virtually continuous trade negotiations as, successively, the EU's internal market 1992 project, the Canada–USA and then NAFTA agreement, and finally the Uruguay Round deals were forged (Doern, Pal, and Tomlin, 1996).

The free trade model not only shifted the power centres interested in, and involved with, industrial policy and, by extension, intellectual property, it also tended to shift the rhetorical packaging and content of policy towards 'international competitiveness' or similarly named strategies. Such policies focused on the broader and more generic aspects of all of a country's factors of production. Thus the need to pay attention to capital investment, natural resources, human capital and education and knowledge came to the fore (with knowledge being not only R&D in the traditional sense but also IP and various aspects of innovation) (Nelson, 1993). For economists this seemed like simply an old-fashioned rediscovery of growth theory but in the actual world of microeconomic policy formation, this did mark a change and it involved an ever widening array of ministerial portfolios.

Competitiveness or similarly named strategies were also characterised by a reduced reliance on spending and an increased reliance on the role of knowledge and information. If governments could not spend and subsidise (deficits and new trade rules made these less useable policy instruments) then western governments' industry and trade ministries would have to focus more on supplying knowledge to their business communities. And given the revolution in Internet telecommunications and information technologies, governments would have to become very nimble at such value-added knowledge roles.

A final feature of trade-related competitiveness strategies was that they were also targeted at small and medium-sized businesses to a far greater extent than were the older traditional kinds of industrial policy. In part, this was because of the growth of the small business lobby but also it was because small business was the fastest growing job creator. Moreover, small and medium-sized businesses were less likely to be exporters and hence it was precisely such firms which governments hoped could become exporters if encouraged with the right mix of policies and information.

The emergence of intellectual property policy within a continuum of innovation/competitiveness actions

The first two developments, the decline of traditional industrial policy and the emergence of trade-related policies, are traceable with hindsight but they do not yield a simple causal path for intellectual property policy or for IP institutions. What has happened over the latter stages of these two periods is that governments increasingly saw intellectual property as itself being an integrated overall policy field (Consumer and Corporate Affairs, 1990; Prime Minister's Science and Engineering Council, 1994). At an elementary level this simply meant that intellectual property policy could be described as an amalgam of patent, trademark, copyright and design policies. But was it any more than just an eclectic amalgam of categories?

In part, IP was becoming a more genuine field of overall policy in the sense that competitiveness frameworks were causing both governments and firms to canvass more widely for the keys to modern prosperity and profitability and hence both the value of IP protection and the need to access other people's IP became more appreciated (Best, 1990; Knight, 1995). However, IP was not a policy field that had seamless boundaries. Indeed, the loose notion of competitiveness and the realisation that a vast range of actions were involved in producing innovation (public and private) meant that boundaries were blurring. For example, successful countries and firms could become more innovative depending upon how they handled issues such as: competition policies and enforcement; access to risk capital; cooperative R&D; close relationships with contractors and subcontractors in product and process designs; language skills in foreign markets; investments in in-plant training (Nelson, 1993). IP policy and, equally, various IP services, regulations and actions are a part of this elongated continuum of actions that might potentially be needed to produce competitive firms and nations (Porter, 1990).

But these features were also cast over a period where a goods trading economy was the dominant assumption and reality. The question increasingly arose about what might be different when one related these changes to the new realities of a so-called knowledge economy.

Economists lead the way in the theoretical discussion of these changes, with thinking taking many forms and organising concepts. First, at one level, some economists caution against thinking that growth is now more knowledge based than in the past (Howitt, 1996). They point to frequent earlier historical periods where then new dominant technologies and organisational innovations (textiles, agriculture, autos) were analysed as being crucial determinants of growth.

But many are turning their attention to a reexamination of growth theory with a focus on endogenous growth. This is because earlier simpler aggregate growth theory treated knowledge and technology much like they were 'just another good, capable of being accumulated like capital and aggregated with the same precision (or lack of precision) as capital' (Howitt, 1996, p. 9). Endogenous growth theory has questioned and researched the way in which knowledge is different from goods and hence must be thought about differently in crucial matters of exchange in markets and information that either markets or governments might use to assess knowledge-based development (de la Mothe and Paquet, 1996).

At a more aggregate level, other economists have argued that countries must be looked at as national innovation systems whose features range across many policy fields and activities, from systems of human capital formation to levels of competition (Nelson, 1993). Quasi-populist authors such as Michael Porter also argued for much more catholic views of what combinations of factors contributed to the competitiveness of nations (Porter, 1990).

At this point we simply note the conceptual links between IP, efforts to conceive of it as a more integrated field, and the broader competitiveness-innovation frameworks. We are interested in them mainly because they are influencing policies and IP institutions in the jurisdictions being examined. But this becomes an important issue as well in Chapter 4 when we discuss the protection versus the dissemination roles, particularly the latter, since they run headlong into the denser range of innovative activities and which policy institutions within government ought to focus on their implementation.

Copyright, IP and US policy leadership and political aggressiveness

In the analysis thus far copyright issues and structures have scarcely been mentioned. Our focus has been on the core patent institutions. This will remain true in the analysis as a whole but there is clearly one overall sense in which copyright issues must be emphasised in the present survey of policy change. This is that copyright concerns were at the centre of the US intellectual property agenda and that an IP agenda was in turn central to the trade-in-services thrust that motivated the 'aggressive unilateralism' of US foreign economic policy in the last decade (Bhagwati and Patrick, 1990; Drake and Nicolaidis, 1992; Doremus, 1996).

This is not to suggest that patents were not also a key US concern but it was the copyright issues linked to overall problems of pirating (especially by key developing countries) that became a central part of the US agenda (Sell, 1995; Aoki, 1996; Drahos, 1997). These areas in turn were a part of the larger breakthroughs that the USA sought in trade-in services. This US pressure to liberalise had taken a particularly concerted form in the Canada–USA free trade negotiations (Doern and Tomlin, 1991) but was simultaneously a crucial part of the Uruguay Round. The pressure for breakthroughs in the service sector also came within the US business community from the service industries (Hoekman and Kostecki, 1995). Services were also inextricably bound up in the computer and telecommunications revolution and hence in the emergence of the Internet or information highway where intellectual property issues were extremely complicated and important (Drake, 1995; US Information Infrastructure Task Force, 1995).

It is not difficult to see that these linked issues were in total bound up in the new debates and strategies about competitiveness and about how nations, in an information/knowledge economy, innovate and continuously learn. Within the US Government, as in other western countries, this meant that trade policy ministries were driving agendas. And in the USA there was a direct link between this central fact and the appointment of a copyright expert, Bruce A. Lehman, to head up the USPTO. As already noted, Lehman was to spend large amounts of his time as the Clinton Administration's main IP trade adviser. Within the US Administration, it also meant that copyright policy shifted to the Office of the US Trade Representative, aided by the USPTO and away from its previous centre which was in the Register of Copyright located in the Library of Congress, a legislative branch agency rather than an executive agency. From the late 1980s to the present, the main copyright expertise shifted out of the domain of the Register of Copyright. The latter still retains the important registry function required by US law but policy and political power on copyrights has clearly shifted.

There is a direct link then between these shifts and strategies and the US Government's growing dissatisfaction with the previously mentioned slow pace of decision making within WIPO and the traditional international IP processes. The USA still wanted WIPO to carry out its important functions but it began looking for other institutions to solve the problems identified in its aggressive trade-in services and IP agenda. Because it was copyright centred, the concern was with whether other countries in the world had proper copyright rules and, equally, enforcement provisions. For this, the USA saw the trade policy arena, and the emerging World Trade Organization (WTO) and its hoped for more effective dispute settlement capacities, as its preferred venue. The Uruguay Round's wide ranging negotiations also enabled more pressure to be put on developing countries because wider kinds of trade-offs could be negotiated, including things that developing countries might seek in exchange for providing tougher IP regimes (Bradley, 1987; Beier and Schricker, 1989; Braga, 1995).

As Chapter 8 shows, the TRIPs provisions of the Uruguay Round both consolidate and incorporate older patent and trademark conventions but they also include the long sought US-levered provisions on dispute settlement in the IP field (Trebilcock and Howse, 1995).

This US influence in crucial IP politics is vital in understanding the overall IP institutions of the 1990s, but it is important to note that it did not, in some total sense, turn the operations of the national and international patent offices on their heads. The latter still had their basic examination and registration jobs to do even while knowing that IP issues were being raised to levels of unprecedented political and economic priority.

Conclusions

This chapter has examined the evolution of IP organisations, first, through an account of how their basic governing structures have evolved in the 1990s and, second, by linking these features to the place of IP policy in the industrial and economic policy priorities of national governments. With respect to overall structure, there is an obvious need to appreciate the different dynamics of international bodies, such as WIPO and EPO, where nation states are the members of their governing bodies and where decision processes have been necessarily slow and consensual. The differences between WIPO and EPO have also been emphasised particularly regarding the fact that the representatives on the EPO are typically the heads of national patent offices with a strong sensitivity to the competitive needs of their own institutions.

Regarding the governing structures of national offices, the analysis has shown the need to link the older crucial concept of the 'statutory person' model of regulatory mode with the more recent common changes to establish patent agencies as reinvented executive agencies with greater financial independence and a more service-oriented culture. The chapter has also shown the varied ways in which the policy function has been managed between the operational agencies and the parent policy department, especially industry departments.

The governing structure of IP institutions has also been related to four interwoven developments in the place of IP policy in national and international economic policy priorities. The first two are fairly clear but gradual developments, namely the decline of traditional industrial policy and the ascendancy of trade-related competitiveness strategies and policies. The third is much more subtle. This is that IP policy is seen to be more important than in previous decades, yet it is but one part of what may be a more seamless web of public and private actions needed to yield innovation in a modern knowledge economy rather than just a traditional goods economy.

Finally, the analysis has drawn special attention to the way in which copyright policy within IP has been central to the aggressive unilateralism of US trade policy and strategy. We have shown how this was linked to changes in the IP and trade policy machinery of the US Government and how these changes have reached out to affect international IP bodies such as WIPO by giving prominence to the WTO and its dispute settlement disciplines under the TRIPs agreement.

CHAPTER FOUR

Patents, the Protection Role and Core IP Interests

The protection role is central to the existence of the intellectual property agencies being examined. They exist to establish rights to intellectual property, to creations of the mind. In this chapter we examine the protection role through the prism of four issues or processes:

1   the quality and efficiency of pendency performance or of the central processes of examining patents;
2   issues and debates regarding the length and quality of patent protection and IP protection in general and issues regarding petty patents and 'second-tier protection';
3   the role of big business in giving focus to the protection function;
4   the role of the IP professions as intermediary interests between inventors and the IP agencies but whose primary interest is also in the protection function.

In clustering these business and professional interests around the protection role the intention is not to suggest that they have no interest or stake in the dissemination roles to be examined in Chapter 5. They do. Indeed, it must be reiterated that a crucial form of IP dissemination occurs at precisely the same moment that a patent is approved. The invention is simultaneously being protected and made public because the alternative for the inventor or inventing firm is always that it could have kept its invention secret. But the essence of the process, once started, is to seek protection and thus there are good reasons for a chapter-length focus on the key features of protection and on the central interests for whom this is the driving force behind their behaviour in dealing with the various national and international agencies.

As is the case throughout this book, the chapter cannot deal with every feature and nuance of the agencies being studied. Accordingly, we seek to examine trends and illustrate the main practices and debates across the jurisdictions, keeping in mind the differences between national and international bodies.

In terms of understanding essential institutional features of the protection role there are several reasons for selecting the issues listed. The first centres on pendency rates or on the basic processes of examination and approval. Thus, in this case we are assuming an existing set of laws and practices and how the IP agency processes its 'case load', so to speak, within these laws. This is an efficiency (time and cost) issue but it also involves crucial aspects of the quality of regulation (time and technical validity and capacity) since the patent must have integrity and validity.

These core processing aspects are also bound up in the agency's financial 'essence', since it is on both initial and renewal fees for patents and trademarks that the agency is increasingly or even totally dependent. And it is in the sharing of fees that crucial relationships between national and international bodies are founded, both cooperative and competitive relationships.

In a closely related feature of the protection role, the discussion shifts to the length and quality of the protection afforded. This entails a look at pressures to change the legal basis of the length of protection (the situation in recent years) but there is more involved here than this (Trebilcock and Howse, 1995, Chapter 10). For example, in some jurisdictions the issue of shorter term and less rigorous utility models or petty patents arise. Differences also arise between developing and developed countries over the length and nature of protection (Rapp and Rozak, 1990). There can also be sectoral differences within industry. Finally, there are issues concerning the relationship between competition laws and policies, which are intended to promote competition, and intellectual property law, some features of which are intended to create monopolies, and other features of which are to promote innovation (Niosi, 1995; Doern and Wilks, 1996).

Pendency, efficiency and agency revenues

Under the pressure of increasingly globalised trade and competition all of the national offices have paid increasing attention to lowering their pendency rates and to making them their central operational performance criteria. These criteria go by different names in different national IP offices but in the case of the USA, the pendency rate is the average time in months from filing to either issuance or abandonment of a patent application (US Patent and Trademark Office, 1994, p. 9 and p. 79). A central focus in recent years has been to improve these performance features in part because they have been linked to the growing trend to finance national offices almost totally from the fees earned and to reduce government tax-based financing to zero. The logic here was unassailable. If businesses and inventors (but mainly big business) were paying the way, they wanted improved performance. Faster – but effective and valid – patent approvals became the order of the day. Computerised and automated processes were also making it possible to handle large and complex kinds of information more efficiently.

In the USPTO, the largest of the national offices being examined, the pressure for increased performance dated back to the early to mid-1980s. The USPTO already styled itself, as one official put it, as 'Detroit with paper', and hence it was geared to be an efficient patent examining assembly line operation. In the early 1980s the movement which saw (increased) fees go from about 50 percent to 80 percent of revenues was sold to American business and to the IP legal profession on the promise that pendency rates would improve. And pendency rates did improve to the targeted (promised) range of 18 months.

Countries varied in the degree to which their IP agencies were prepared to commit in detail to such basic performance criteria and to be bound by them. Moreover, there is often a reluctance to express them as a single pendency indicator. For example, the Australian Industrial Property Organization (AIPO) indicates in its 1995–99 business plan that it seeks to increase the processing of patent filings from 40,615 in 1995–96 to 49,385 in 1997–98 and 54,365 in 1998–99. But these targets for each year are then broken down into subtasks such as 'provisionals, completes, designations, and petty patent applications' (Australian Industrial Property Organization, 1995, pp. 10–11).

Both special agency status, and the pressure for published service standards in government reform, caused the agencies to be ever more aware of this central engine of their existence. However, they were also aware of the many factors which could affect performance. For example, the USPTO's basic pendency rate has increased in recent years to 19.5 in fiscal year 1993 and then down somewhat to 19.0 in 1994. This slippage has been attributed to three causes. First, some of the newer technological areas such as computers and biotechnologies produce patent applications which are on average longer to process because the examinations are inherently more complex or involve the need for newer staff. Second, despite special operating status, there have been significant cuts in personnel which simply slows the pace of examinations on average. Third, Clinton era administrative reform, including further personnel cuts, have been applied in a classic across-the-board fashion and thus, even growing agencies with demonstrated growth in demand such as the USPTO has experienced, have had cuts applied to them. As we saw in Chapter 3, these are among the factors that have prompted the demand for a full government corporation status for the USPTO.

As soon as the pressures on one country for such core pendency rates (and for the fee structures around them) are described the pressure on other national offices follows quickly but also in varied ways. The fact that the USPTO was pressured to improve its performance is important simply because it is arguably the most dynamic IP-oriented economy. Thus, US performance increases had an immediate impact in Canada where CIPO was under pressure because both firms and the patent profession in Canada, which knew both systems, could point to the slower Canadian pendency performance. They protested accordingly to CIPO and have maintained the pressure in their regular meetings with CIPO officials.

In another sense, one could look at the USA and simply argue that the USPTO has nothing to worry about regarding its performance because after all it has a monopoly within the USA and it has a huge and growing IP market as more and more firms use IP as part of their competitive strategies. The cost of getting a patent in the USA is about one-tenth the cost of getting a patent from the European Patent Office. The reasons for the EPO's high costs are discussed further later but, despite their cost advantage, the USPTO is aware that in the not too distant future there will likely be more direct and real competition in the offering of patent and IP services. The pressure for change is already coming from big multinational businesses to have a system that is virtually a one-stop harmonised patent process. USPTO officials already indicate that some business surveys of EPO patents indicate, despite or perhaps because of higher EPO costs, that they are of a higher quality than some types of US patent services. Full harmonisation has of course many hurdles to overcome, not the least of which is US conversion from a 'first to invent' to a 'first to file' system.

Before considering the EPO's strength as a potential global competitor, it is best to enter the European pendency rate domain through the venue of the UK Patent Office. The UK Patent Office's desire for improved performance is driven by similar global forces and by the freedoms and disciplines inherent in its executive agency status. But it is the presence and policies of the EPO that most drives the strategies of the UK office. Sixty percent of the UK Patent Office's revenue now comes from patents but since 1978, the EPO has taken away about 50 percent of its core patent business. There are, of course, advantages for UK businesses if they can obtain a patent from the EPO because it confers wider multi-country coverage within the European countries named in the application. The UK Patent Office also obtains, as do other EPO member countries, half of the EPO's renewal fee income.

The EPO's pendency processes and fee structures were partly based on the logic of its start-up period (in the 1970s and early 1980s) and partly on the delicate politics of its relationships with member countries and national patent offices. The EPO's initial fees had to be quite high relative to national offices simply because it did not have a set of existing patents on which it could earn renewal fees. Had it had renewal fee income, it could have had lower front-end charges. Gradually, it did obtain a stream of renewal fee income and its fees came down. However, its fees are very much higher than UK fees (and US and Canadian fees) largely because:

- there are extensive language translation costs that have to be absorbed;
- patent applications are examined by three examiners rather than one;
- the EPO has a much higher salary and pension system for its international civil servants compared to its national office equivalents;
- there are pressures from its members with full national patent offices that the EPO not lower its prices in such a way that it puts remaining national offices out of business.

The EPO relationship with a national office such as the UK Patent Office is both a cooperative and competitive one. The UK Patent Office sees itself as a more cost-effective operation and indeed sees itself as supplying a benchmark comparison for, and discipline on, an international bureaucracy which would otherwise have an even more bloated cost structure. But, at the same time, it must watch carefully, as a fully fee-dependent agency, exactly what the pattern of EPO business is likely to be in the coming years, both in terms of initial and renewal fees. The trademark side of the UK Patent Office will have to similarly adapt its work in the light of the new European Trademark Office at Alicante, Spain. Thus, for the foreseeable future, Europe's IP institutions will have two distinct bureaucracies, one for patents and the other for trademarks, with all the attendant additional overhead operational costs (compared to the USPTO or national offices in Europe).

But what looks like bloated costs from one jurisdiction's perspective can simply be the *real politik* when seen from the vantage point of a functioning international body. The USA and the UK both function in a national single language economy. The EPO must function in a political-economic context in which the language of commerce is not a small matter.

The EPO's more expensive and time-consuming process for examinations is partly due to language needs but also because harmonisation had to occur among the different national systems it was replacing/augmenting. There also had to be trust built up in the quality and validity of the judgements. Three examiner processes were accordingly the norm. The informal target standard for performance on the cost side is that an EPO patent will cost no more than the cost of obtaining the same patent in three separate member countries.

Just as the USA is eyeing the costs of the EPO patent, so the EPO is aware of its greater costs vis-à-vis the US. At present an EPO cost study is underway. It is looking at the cost of a defined standard EPO patent (e.g. involving an eight-country coverage, translation into six languages and other criteria). It is estimated that the direct costs of such a patent are about DM20,000, of which three-quarters is attributable to translation costs. The pressure from industry in Europe is to lower these costs greatly (perhaps to as low as DM4000 which means lowering/eliminating some or major aspects of translation costs. Some firms are already shopping around various national offices in Europe to obtain the best costing advantages. Meanwhile, the European patent profession opposes such cost reduction measures, often because, in some member countries, the translation aspects of the business are in fact the bread and butter of their IP-related business.

The EPO has also argued with its member states (and their national IP offices) that it should get a higher proportion (as high as 75 percent versus the current 50 percent) of the EPO renewal fees. Had it more renewal fee income, the EPO could reduce its initial fees. This idea has been resisted by member states, especially those with national offices concerned about their own viability in the face of EPO competition.

WIPO is the final agency to be examined in the basic patent examination and approval process. As pointed out in Chapter 2, WIPO does not grant patents but it is a crucial player through the vehicle of the Patent Cooperation Treaty (PCT) which vastly enhances the efficiency of the search and registration aspects of the worldwide patent decision and information process. WIPO and the EPO have a cooperative and competitive relationship, in that the EPO is the biggest search and examination office for the PCT.

But the PCT must first be seen in the context of WIPO. In essence, the PCT 'funds the house' as one WIPO official put it. The PCT is a filing system that supplies 85 percent of WIPO's income. In recent years PCT fees have been very buoyant but earlier in the early 1980s this was not the case and accordingly WIPO faced internal financial difficulties. As mentioned in Chapter 3, WIPO is one of the better run UN agencies but there was little doubt that it was facing financial difficulties.

One area that suffered the brunt of this period of financial constraint was WIPO's work in propagating IP knowledge and institutions in developing countries. However, by the late 1980s and certainly in the 1990s, the use of the PCT increased markedly as businesses saw its advantages. Accordingly, WIPO's income increased greatly. This produced a remarkable confluence of income and perceived need. The needs of developing countries in IP exploded in the 1990s, especially with the need to conform to new TRIPs and other provisions. Instead of having to pry the costs of these developmental project-like funds out of reluctant member state contributions, WIPO was able to argue that the support should come directly out of basic PCT income. The argument was simply that the business applicant that used the PCT had a legitimate stake in ensuring that appropriate IP regimes and practices were present in as broad a range of countries as possible and hence they should directly help pay for this work. Accordingly, a portion of the fee income has been so ear-marked.

WIPO must, of course, pay first for its basic ability to run the PCT system. But again PCT growth has been such that WIPO has become a relatively prosperous UN agency endowed with sufficient revenues that, on its own, it has been able to take further related decisions, such as those needed to computerise its operations further. Indeed, its relative financial buoyancy has attracted the attention of the financial hawks among its member countries. Chief among these has been the USA, but also the EPO which has raised concerns about the costs of WIPO's operations, particularly given its expensive Geneva base. The USA has suggested that some operations be shifted to San Francisco where some costs could be reduced markedly.

The central engine of the patent examination and approval process obviously drives the agencies sampled here and is increasingly linked both to agency finances and to the cooperative and competitive strategies of national and international IP institutions. There are some parallel developments in the trademark area as well, since typically this is the second largest area of business. These have not been discussed here but aspects of the institutional links between patents and trademarks will emerge in Chapter 6 and in our overview of the role of business and of the IP profession.

Length and quality of protection

The earlier discussion has been premised on an assumption that we were dealing with operations within a more or less given set of laws. However, the protection role of IP institutions writ large is also affected by pressures and issues to change the basic length or quality of the protection in laws and treaties. The pace at which this has been done has increased greatly in recent years and thus is itself an indicator of the degree to which IP is a growing concern in governmental and business strategies for growth in a knowledge-based information economy. The seven agencies provide a further window into these aspects of the protection function.

The first and most important aspect has been the achievement in the Uruguay Round of a harmonised patent of 20 years duration (from filing date). The length of patent protection is an issue replete with both economic and political calculation and pressure. A simple question is 'Why 20 years?', another 'Why one period for all industrial sectors or kinds of invention?'. The answers are more complex and, in fact, lead to conclusions which show that protections are actually not that long or rigid.

Patents are intended to produce a temporary monopoly to reward intellectual effort and ingenuity. But simple economic logic suggests that these periods of protection ought to vary greatly by field or sector depending on varying cost structures, investments, and payback periods. As we saw in Chapter 1, this also suggests that countries would have different views about what kinds of protection across sectors would make the most sense given their national state of development and strategies for development. Thus the underlying economics of patent protection suggests the suitability of many periods of protection and that these could also change over time.

However, the political and institutional logic is somewhat different. It goes as follows. First, for key players the basic logic is simply the longer the protection period the better. This view is driven by firms such as those in the national and global pharmaceutical and biotechnology industries who seek out maximum effective protection. Their desire for maximum periods is driven by factors such as high upfront costs in R&D and in obtaining ever lengthening drug approval processes by other government regulators in several countries. In the 1980s they saw their effective protection being reduced due to the combined effects of patent approval delays and slow drug approval processes, and sought change in national laws and trade regimes. The 'longer is better' logic was also the driving force behind the USA, and later the European Union, in successive trade negotiations. US power was crucial in this regard in that the Americans saw IP as increasingly crucial for US economic development and related it both to developing countries with weaker regimes on patents but also to similarly developed countries such as Canada which it pressured to change its patent laws as well (Trebilcock and Howse, 1995). In Canada, this pressure focused on preferences given to generic drug manufacturers and was brought to bear both before and during successive FTA, NAFTA and GATT negotiations (Doern and Tomlin, 1991).

In the last decade, in particular, there were few if any effective counterpressures from those interests/countries that might have made the counterarguments. Developing countries mounted some counterpressure but were eventually worn down by more powerful forces. Consumers in some overall sense had a vested interest in less monopolistic practices but, at both national and certainly at international levels, they were a weak, diffused, virtually voiceless interest. Perhaps the only exception to this was in the health sector where health ministries were often a surrogate representative of consumer or patient interests.

And last but hardly least, the logic of longer protection periods and for one long period also came from the political and administrative logic of trade negotiations and implementation. It was simply easier to agree on one such longish period because it would be easier to implement. Moreover, it would preserve the notion that IP was indeed an area of real framework law which applied across the economies of member states and did not constitute a form of sector-specific 'industrial' policy which it would be if many sectoral-based periods of protection were possible.

All of this political-economic logic could also be justified in some overall sense because IP institutions knew that patents in many sectors were not maintained over anything like 20 years. On average patents lapsed (that is, were not renewed or maintained through renewal fees) after about 7 to 10 years, depending on the country.

The second more specific illustration of the issue of the length and quality of patents is bound up in policies and practices regarding utility models, petty patents, short-term patents or what is often labelled more generally as 'second-tier protection'. Many countries have such forms of lesser protection, with the IP regime characterised broadly by a lower level of inventiveness, shorter terms of protection, and limits on scope, the coverage of technologies and the number of claims. Second-tier protection regimes have been growing in recent years in that some 48 countries have such systems today compared to only eleven in 1978 (Advisory Council on Industrial Property, 1995, p. 21). Countries such as Germany and Japan have had utility model protection for decades whereas the UK and Canada have not adopted such a system.

Recent developments in the jurisdictions being examined are illustrative of the shifting political economy of IP concerns. For example, the Commission of the European Union has released a green paper on this subject. It is a larger EU, as distinct from an EPO, concern in that utility models are the preferred IP regime in some EU countries such as Spain and Italy but at the same time, national systems are different and hence problems are raised regarding the integrity of the internal market of the EU. The EU, as we saw earlier, also has a broader industrial or innovation policy mandate for European industry as a whole in that it is concerned that European industry is lagging behind its major US and Japanese competitors (European Patent Office, 1994).

The dilemmas of second-tier protection were illustrated in a 1994 symposium sponsored in the UK by the UK patent profession, the Chartered Institute of Patent Agents. Various approaches were put forward ranging from an EU-wide regulation, as advocated by the Max Planck Institute, to a national UK system. The case for second-tier protection centred first on whether there was a case at all for providing protection for technical innovation that had some merit but which was several notches below that required for a full patent. Many UK practitioners were suspicious of the value of this approach, in part because the UK simply did not have one. Other professionals and officials involved, particularly those focusing on how to get smaller firms involved in, and aware of IP, saw merit in second-tier protection.

Invariably, the next issue of import was that, if valid, such a system would then have to be more quickly, simply, and cheaply available than full patents were. At the same time, such a system could not be, or be seen to be, harmful to the integrity of the already established patent regimes. In a European context, there were already cost concerns at an EU level because of the issue of translation costs. The Max Planck Institute proposal had proposed very restricted translation provisions, precisely to keep costs down. But such restrictions would be politically unacceptable among some EU countries and their IP professions.

Australia provides a further example of recent moves for second-tier protection. Australia has a petty patent system but, nonetheless, a 1995 study recommended that a further 'innovation patent system' be put in place. The impetus for the study came from the small business lobby with the study requested by the Minister for Small Business, Customs and Construction. The innovation patent was to fill the gap 'between designs and standard patents' and would have to have the other features referred to earlier, namely speed, cheapness of cost, simplicity, and, as well a 'measure of certainty' to encourage 'investment in the developing and marketing of innovation' especially by small and medium-sized businesses (Advisory Council on Industrial Property, 1995, p. 5).

The third issue concerning the length and quality of protection can be seen as simultaneously sectoral and/or a concern related to a country's view of its 'state of economic development'. Among nations (developed and developing, among developed, among developing) there can and will be different judgements about which sectors of comparative advantage each possesses. These differences have affected debates in a north–south context in the TRIPs negotiations and are examined later in this chapter in the discussion of enforcement and the WTO. But, meanwhile, sectoral dynamics are themselves a variable in the protection equation.

Each of the national and international offices has faced problems of adjustment as new families of technology/invention occur and come on the scene. These show up with the IP agency in terms of the need to recruit examiners with the right technical expertise but an expertise which is arguably more cross-disciplinary than in the past.

Pharmaceuticals have been a source of such change but in recent years it has been in areas such as biotechnology and computer and information sciences where adaptive problems have been greatest. Adaptation is needed not only in simply acquiring the right people (in a fiercely competitive and high salaried professional labour market) but it is also the case that, because these sciences and their products are complex, case applications and examinations can take longer, pendency performance can be slowed, and oppositions and litigation may increase.

Beyond these broad changes, there are also wider arrays of institutions involved which may have a say in how these issues are resolved at a basic policy level or even on individual cases. For example, in recent years the negotiations about intellectual property rights in the biotechnology area have been bounded as well by discussions among environmental institutions on matters such as biodiversity. Negotiations were occurring simultaneously in the mid-1990s in the WTO–TRIPs arena and in the Biodiversity Convention process (Purdue, 1995). The US Government, pressured heavily by the US Biotechnology Association, the main business lobby in the field, took steps to ensure that any biodiversity provisions were made subordinate to the intellectual property provisions of TRIPs (Purdue, 1995, p. 102).

The fourth aspect of the length and quality of protection centres on the broad links between national and international competition laws on the one hand, and IP laws on the other (Gallini and Trebilcock, 1996; Anderman, 1998; Maher, 1998). IP law creates and endorses monopolies and, in a strict sense, is anticompetitive. Competition law exists to promote competition among firms and economic entities. How then do the laws and institutions of the two realms relate to each other? Which law prevails? Or how are they accommodated or fudged? Space allows us only a few basic observations about these links across the jurisdictions being examined.

First, it would appear that national IP institutions broadly believe that their realms have precedence and that it is competition law and policy that is 'fenced out' and deemed not in general to apply to situations where intellectual property rights *per se* apply. Second, competition laws themselves vary across the jurisdictions as to whether their sole or main purpose is competition as such or is linked to related economic concepts such as:

- consumer surplus (a stronger norm in the USA);
- economic efficiency (the case in Canada);
- economic integration (the situation in the EU);
- broader public interest or even industrial policy objectives (the situation in the UK) (Doern and Wilks, 1996).

They also vary in their enforcement mechanisms including whether private actions are possible.

However, in the 1990s, it would appear that concerns about institutional links between the each separately desirable areas of marketplace framework policy are growing. For example, in the US debate about the possible location of the USPTO if the Department of Commerce were abolished, there was strong opposition in the USPTO to its being located in the Justice Department for fear that it would run headlong into a culture dominated by that department's aggressive antitrust division. This was certainly a manifestation of a larger potential for cases in which IP issues and competition issues would and had already collided under the US system where private actions are the norm in antitrust matters. For example cases of anticompetitive behaviour have involved situations where patented products or production processes (themselves protected under IP law) were being extended into anticompetitive actions through the vehicle of licensing arrangements or particular aspects of these arrangements.

In the USA and elsewhere, the more that IP is viewed politically and economically as the 'new protectionism', with IP becoming the 'high tariff' of the knowledge and information economy, the more that antitrust cases will be mounted to test the real limits of both sets of laws. Which is fenced out of where will be a more fluid, debatable and contested concept.

To demonstrate a further aspect of these relationships, it is also necessary to look at practices intended to encourage cooperative R&D and technological alliances among firms. Governments in all of the jurisdictions being surveyed have encouraged such alliances and indeed have taken various measures to exempt such activities from the threat of possible antitrust actions. At the same time, when it comes to obtaining patents for such collaborative work there are still severe difficulties in part because fears of antitrust action still remain and in part because it is genuinely difficult to define property rights and which parties to the alliance should hold them or seek them from IP institutions (Niosi, 1995). Given that such alliances are frequently international in nature, the problems presented can be even greater.

All of these examples suggest that issues concerning the length and quality of protection will continue to be important to the national and international IP agencies being studied. They will also likely become more contested and thus test the limits of the degree to which IP laws can be kept as framework versus sectorally varied laws, institutions and practices.

Big business and the protection role

Many business firms – small, medium and large – seek intellectual property rights but it is big business, and in particular, large multinational firms, that are most crucial in understanding the core protection role (Warshovsky, 1994). Mention will be made of small and medium-sized enterprises but they are more fully examined in Chapter 5. It must be stressed that no IP agency suggests publically that big business is its primary clientele. If anything, as we have seen, agency descriptions of their clientele or customers, range across a broad array of inventors or businesses, including the individual person as inventor, the ultimate, almost populist vision of an enterprise and innovating culture and economy.

However, it should be no surprise that big business in many ways drives the IP agenda and the protection function. The large chemical and pharmaceutical firms (US, European and Japanese) have by far the biggest stake in an efficient, effective and valid patent system. They have been joined in recent years by firms in the biotechnology and computer industries and now in the more amorphous fast changing telecommunications and information service industries, the latter including the banks and financial institutions, who are among the fastest growing users of the IP system (US Information Infrastructure Task Force, 1995). On the copyright side, big businesses include media, entertainment and recording industries with vast lobbying resources, especially in the USA.

In pointing out this influence, and its intensification under the pressures of globalisation, one is not describing some simple version of conspiratorial power between IP agencies and big business. The basis of the relationship is more multidimensional and subtle than that and hence its roots must be understood in the context both of the present chapter and Chapter 5. First, the relationship is a functional one inherent in capitalism itself. Governments depend on business as the major job creators and as the major sources of innovation. Second, the influence of big businesses is based on superior lobbying resources, nationally and internationally, with a far greater capacity to mobilise at the international level. Indeed, at the international level, their own direct lobbying with the agencies is augmented by their own government's membership in the international agencies since a nation's national IP offices are most concerned either with their own large firms or with a desire to attract incoming investment. In considering the sources of business power it is important to stress that it does not come just from their national or international interest groups but also from the firms themselves working on their own in the counsels of national governments at the bureaucratic and ministerial levels. This is why it is crucial to define IP institutions as going beyond the IP agencies themselves to include industry and trade ministries.

A third source of the influence of big business is that no other single interest, save that of the IP profession (see later) has the organisational staying power to interact almost daily with IP agencies. As Chapter 5 will show, small and medium-sized businesses and their interest groups have greater difficulty in being represented, especially in a way that focuses on IP as opposed to a host of other industrial policy concerns. Other interests such as consumers or environmental interests are usually too diffuse for sustained influence. Various advisory bodies have been established around the IP agencies to ensure that a broader array of clients are advising the agencies. These are discussed in Chapter 5 where our focus is on the efforts of the IP agencies to become more service oriented. But our concern in this chapter is with the basis of big business leverage as both an interest group and as the dominant customer.

One variation on this theme to note, however, is that of business interests and the trademark realm of IP. Trademarks are certainly a concern of big businesses and multinational firms but, on average, the trademark area is more likely also to involve more medium and small firms. The business interests in this IP realm are also more likely to be seeking and thinking about trademarks only in national terms. Chapter 6 discusses this point in the larger context of the trademark registration process.

A fourth source of the big business influence arises from the fact that so much of the IP debate is often cast as a technical debate. The IP agencies have seen themselves, quite rightly in most respects, as technically competent regulatory bodies performing an important operational function in a politically neutral manner. This sense of technical neutrality has been aided by the more recent even greater emphasis on the need for agencies to implement good framework marketplace law that is sector neutral.

Thus in saying that big business has a privileged place in the IP agency–business relationship as a whole, the argument here is not that other segments of business receive no attention. But an institutional perspective has to include a good sense of the basic relationships of power in any regulatory system.

The first three parts of this chapter and earlier discussion together indicate other important instances where big business influence is in evidence. First, in the realm of pendency rates and the new fee-based financing of IP agencies, there is little doubt that major firms, that see themselves as global competitors, are the main source of pressure to improve pendency rates. Indeed, it could be argued that the more that fees are the only source of agency income the more that business in general, and big businesses in particular, will want to call more of the tune. In the USA, the debate over whether there should be a new corporate version of the USPTO and, if so, what its governing structure should be, is largely split along big business versus small business and small inventor interest group coalitions. The pressure to reduce the costs and the time periods of EPO patents is also coming from both European and US multinational firms.

With respect to changes to the length of patents and with regard to copyright enforcement and trade-related measures, there is no doubt at all that the engine of change is large multinational firms which are focusing their lobbying around trade policy institutions in the USA but quickly finding allies in the EU–EPO as well. It is these business interests, more than any other factor, that forced the changes described earlier in the relationship between WIPO and the WTO.

Even the brief discussion of the debate about petty patents or utility models can be linked to these basic roles of big business versus small business influence. The fact that the establishment of simpler 'second-tier' protection regimes has increased considerably suggests that perhaps small business interests are gaining more leverage because, typically, it is the small firm sector that lobbies for such regimes. It may simply be, however, that this is really an admission that 'first-tier' protection is a big business or largely big business preserve, in short, an IP game that increasingly only a few can play.

The IP profession and the protection role

As is the case with the big business role, our discussion of the place of the IP profession in the protection role of the agencies must be brief and illustrative. Again it is necessary to state that our linking the profession with the protection function is not intended to imply that there is no interest by the profession in the IP dissemination issues which we discuss in Chapter 5.

The first issue is obviously that of defining what the profession is and how is it structured and related to IP agencies. The answer to the first question is that the profession is a diverse one in that in different countries it is a full sub-area or specialty of the legal profession (as in the USA). In others, such as Canada, the UK, Australia and Europe, it is a separate profession of patent agents or attorneys, with trademark agents either a part of the larger profession or separate from it (the case in the UK) (FICPI, 1992; Office of Fair Trading, 1986; Doern, 1995). To further complicate matters, in countries with separate professions, there are many practising professionals who are both members of the bar and members of the IP profession. At the larger international level, regional or worldwide, the profession's presence is reflected in organisations such as the Fédération Internationale des Conseils en

Propriété Industrielle (FICPI) and the International Association for the Protection of Intellectual Property (AIPPI). Here the profession broadens in that membership may also include businesses as such or businesses whose key employees are also members of the profession in their own right.

Another key feature of the profession and of its close links with major IP business firms is the transformation of law firms and the contracting out of IP functions by many large IP firms to law firms. In earlier periods, in most of the countries being examined, the largest firms had their own inhouse stable of patent agents or lawyers. Some of the largest still do. But in general, there had been a tendency for such firms to hand over their patent and other functions to law firms which had developed IP or patent specialties. In recent years, developments in the legal profession more generally has also caused law firms to see IP as a growth area, and hence a business opportunity.

In most respects the IP profession is a relatively lucrative profession requiring extensive technical and legal knowledge. There are, however, some divisions within the profession or among its professional components. For example, the trademark profession is often seen as a secondary area, both in terms of volume of business and level of technical and educational background. The profession as a whole is also characterised by a considerable justifiable sense of professional pride about what it sees as its independent public interest role, as an intermediary between the IP applicant and the state authorities.

In terms of the core protection role of IP agencies, the nature of the relationship between the profession is threefold in nature. First, the profession supplies a realm of expertise and independent competence which, if the profession did not exist, the agency would undoubtedly have to reinvent within the agency to ensure quality control of the application process. Second, for the inventor or IP applicant, the profession supplies an objective and experienced person who can enhance the overall efficiency, quality, and validity of a patent. Third, and at the same time, the inventor or applicant, especially the smaller applicant/business, is in a basic trust relationship with the professional, dependent upon the latter's honesty, expertise and judgement.

Because of these features of mutual dependence between the agency and the profession, the IP agencies have typically been given roles by statute in ensuring or certifying the basic professional qualifications of the profession. Thus, in varying ways the agencies regulate the profession or aspects of the profession (Doern, 1995). The profession lives off the regulatory system in both a public interest and private interest sense, and the profession, especially when seen as large law firms, is also a business.

It is obvious, then, that there is a broad symbiotic relationship between the IP profession and major IP-oriented business firms, both nationally and internationally. But the basis of their influence and interest is somewhat different. The IP profession is in fact a mélange of:

- individual professionals practising their profession; their national and international associations which both lobby for their interests and promote professionalism;
- a set of legal or IP businesses or firms aligned to IP firms and clients.

Accordingly, the profession, because of its own interest and because of its links to bigger IP firms, has also pushed hard for more efficient pendency rates. Like the business interests it is more aware than others of the relative speed and quality of service that might be available in different national offices. At the same time, however, the national IP professions are wary of measures or developments that might take business away from them or their national offices. In this regard, they face pressures not only directly associated with IP policy and regulation but also pressures from changes in trade law which are beginning to encourage freer trade in services, including, of course, professional services.

In many ways, the IP professions have the most regular access to IP agencies on policy and operational matters. Even today, they are likely to be the most numerously represented in the agencies' newly created or strengthened advisory bodies (see Chapter 5). But the profession is also troubled, or at least ambivalent, about the recent institutional changes in many of the IP agencies being examined. The profession focuses on the IP protection role because that is what it knows best and that is how it makes its living. But it increasingly sees IP agencies describing their roles, as we have already seen, in terms of broader IP dissemination roles. The profession does not, in principle, oppose such roles but it is not sure whether this is its role, and whether it will lose or gain economically from them. There is uncertainty, too, about what it might mean if these dissemination roles become the main focus for national offices as broader protection functions 'move up', so to speak, to regional or world IP agencies.

Research for this book has not focused on the professions as such but there are, no doubt, glimpses that do show the mixed pressures at work. All of the professions in the jurisdictions covered are pushing for faster pendency processes often by pressuring their national offices to hire more examiners, and to advance the processes of computerisation. Both Canada and Australia have launched studies or reviews concerning how the agencies ought to be linked to the profession in the new more complex circumstances of the mid- to late 1990s. For some time, and at several levels, the IP profession has been concerned about how its own members can be kept up to date, given the knowledge explosion and the new scientific and technical disciplines from which innovations are emerging.

Conclusions

The protection role is central to the operations of the IP agencies but its institutional features need to be seen in relation to the four issues and processes examined. The protection role is without doubt the central driving force within the IP agencies, despite the recent search for broader IP dissemination functions.

With respect to basic pendency performance and the efficiency and quality of the patent or trademark application process, the chapter shows that there has been an increased pressure, led by large IP firms and industrial interest groups, to improve and make more transparent the performance criteria of such examination and registration operations. This is crucially tied to agency fees and hence agency financial viability as all agencies become executive or special corporate bodies with greater financial freedoms.

Recent years have also seen pressures to change the length and quality of IP protection. The TRIPs negotiations saw the realisation of a harmonised 20-year rule despite other analytical logic which suggests that time periods could vary by sector. At the same time pressures, largely from the small business sector, but building also on different national traditions, saw increased development of utility models and petty patents. These argued for shorter, less expensive, and less rigorous forms of protection. The quality and length of IP protection does not appear to have been directly affected much, in institutional terms, by competition laws but the analysis suggests that these two framework regimes are more likely to collide in the coming years, especially if IP is seen to become internationally the protectionist 'weapon of choice', replacing the tariff, for the world's most powerful firms and nations. Biotechnology inventions and environmental framework laws may also collide more frequently or at least will need a considerable sorting out.

Finally, the chapter shows the tight links between big business interests and the IP professions in the reinforcement of the protection function. Their interests are not identical but it is important to identify both the differences and the similarities in their positions as the dominant interests in the protection role. They bring to the IP agencies, especially under the conditions of globalisation, a strong pressure to improve the efficiency of pendency but also its quality. IP agencies themselves are increasingly seeking to broaden their own sense of their clientele beyond these two primary sets of interests, but, at the same time, they know that they are extremely dependent on one another for the smooth functioning of the central IP protection role.

CHAPTER FIVE

The IP Dissemination Roles and Dispersed Emerging Interests

The IP dissemination role as a whole is both an old and new role for IP institutions and the fourfold structure of this chapter indicates the plurality of issues it now embraces. The chapter also indicates how, at the conjuncture of these issues, there is an array of important but much more varied and dispersed interests than found adjacent to the protection role. First, we look at the oldest IP dissemination role, namely that of making available to IP users in the economy the current information held in the stock of patents, nationally and globally. Second, the chapter examines briefly a further more recent variation on this role in which IP agencies and/or their parent industry ministries see opportunities, through computer information technologies, to make available to business new value-added kinds of commercially useful information from IP information held by the government.

The third section of the chapter deals with IP dissemination in the form of efforts to expand awareness of IP among those parts of the economy and society which have not yet sought IP rights so that more firms will use the IP systems and contribute to a more innovative economy. In some instances, such efforts can be seen as campaigns to produce an IP culture in national economies. Finally, we look in an overall way at the nature of interests and clients involved in these functions. This cluster of interests embraces a much more dispersed array of interests than does the protection role in that small and medium-sized businesses, individual inventors, universities, and fast forming knowledge networks and consulting firms are involved. This does not mean that big business and the IP profession have no stake in these roles. They are also major users of IP information. Rather what happens is that a wider set of interests inherently coalesce around these roles. The roles are more diffuse than the protection role and so are the interests.

As was the case in Chapter 4, care must be taken in differentiating national from international IP agencies in this discussion. For example, in WIPO in particular, the dissemination function is linked closely to a larger education and development role in developing countries. A further qualifying point for IP as a whole is that dissemination issues do not technically apply to copyright in the same way because of the absence of a registration function in the first place and hence they are not discussed here. Chapter 7 shows, however, that there are important issues about the availability of copyrighted material to various commercial and social users, but this is a larger issue that is increasingly linked to the degree to which developments such as the Internet can be regulated as opposed to being seen as an enabling institution that promotes a free exchange of information (Drake, 1995).

One further point about the various kinds of IP dissemination roles is that they must be linked institutionally and politically to the question of who ought to pay for these activities. Should current IP users who have patents or trademarks and who pay for the protection function through their fees also pay for other users, including future users? Or, alternatively, should this be paid from some other source? If it is a general taxpayer source, then the government must maintain a strong say, perhaps more than is recognised by the recent move to special operating agency status and the use of mechanisms of fee-based financial flexibility. Inevitably, such issues also raise questions about the division of labour between national and international IP agencies. For example, one question emerging in the later 1990s is whether national offices that now have full IP functions (protection and dissemination) might devolve into national offices that focus much more, or even exclusively, on IP dissemination roles such as the IP awareness function. But a logical follow-up question is to ask whether such roles can be played out successfully, if a national office does not have the critical mass of a protection function to supply the needed expertise? It may also be asked, if a dissemination role is intricately tied to other aspects of innovation in the modern knowledge economy, whether such roles might not be better carried out by other combined parts of a country's industry department.

IP dissemination I: informing about the current stock of IP information

IP Dissemination I is the oldest dissemination role and flows from the heart of the basic IP policy and public interest trade-off. In exchange for the patent or other IP aspect being protected by the state, the intellectual property information must be made public. Others can use it through commercial arrangements with the patent holders, such as licensing agreements, and they can search and study patents and accompanying information with a view to using them as a base for yet further invention. Hence, aspects of a socially and economically useful innovation chain emerge, nationally and globally (Knight, 1995).

One way of distinguishing IP Dissemination I from IP Dissemination II is that, as seen traditionally, the first of these roles has been practised by IP agencies in a fairly passive public goods-oriented manner. That is, the information is not so much marketed as made available in the same way a public library makes information available. We leave to the next section the issues of just how different a new more aggressive value-added IP dissemination role is but, in the meantime, the nature of this basic role and the interests it serves needs to be sketched out. There are variations across the IP agencies in how this basic IP dissemination role is carried out but, broadly, a similar logic applies.

The first aspect of this logic is that IP information is seen as but one part of a larger stock of information involved in the transfer of technology within nations and among them. In the overall realm of technology transfer, there are massively varied sources and forms of information. However, one of the advantages of IP information, where one million patent documents alone are published worldwide each year, is that 'it is not only accessible to any country in the world but selected information is a reflection of current development of technology in a concise and uniform presentation' (World Intellectual Property Organization, 1995, p. 100).

The second pattern across the national and international agencies is that the basic stock of IP information is used by industry, research and development institutions, universities and governments. Industry is by far the biggest user with again larger firms being the most frequent users within the industrial user category. The other three categories are lesser users but they are important clients of any IP agency. Governments use such information in different policy and operational situations in departments as varied as industry and health. Research and development institutions and universities are frequent users although all of the agencies encounter what they regard as misconceptions about patents in this sector. This misconception is that professors and students engaged in research have somehow formed the view that patents always deal with major breakthroughs and therefore do not relate directly to their narrower research tasks and accordingly patent information is not utilised. Some offices are therefore striving to ensure that universities have access and better use the basic IP information available. WIPO itself, for example, fostered the creation in 1980 of an international association of professors teaching intellectual property.

A third feature of the basic dissemination function is the undoubted influence of computerisation and the rapid use of new information technologies for storage of and access to IP information. The latter include the use of CD-ROM and other technologies. All agencies, in common with virtually every public and corporate institution, have been transforming themselves from a largely paper world to a computerised one. This has improved access to data and has reduced costs on an overall basis but every IP agency has also struggled with exactly what kinds of systems to adopt in a vortex of new technologies. Thus, along with the gains have come complaints from users about adjustment problems as well as the occasional horror story where new systems went badly wrong or simply did not live up to oversold expectations. More is said later about the effect of computerisation and the Internet on the Dissemination II role but, in relation to the basic role being examined here, there is no doubt that it has produced positive benefits.

One other user of the basic IP information should not be forgotten. This is the patent and trademark examiner in each of the national offices and EPO, as well as officers in WIPO involved in search activities. They are primary users, along with the IP profession. For examiners, however, the information and data are crucial to their work at the core of the IP trade-off between protection and dissemination.

The examiner link also raises important issues regarding the dissemination of information to developing countries and also even for developed countries which might have only national patent information offices. This also means that basic dissemination is partially different for an agency such as WIPO. WIPO and other developing country views are broadly that most individual developing countries should not have full national offices that perform both protection and dissemination roles. Such offices are expensive in part because the conventional wisdom is that any such full service office needs a critical mass of about 100 examiners to cover the main areas. But if dissemination offices are needed, a practical dilemma is how one assembles the critical mass of expertise needed to run them. In other words, the examination–protection function in combination is what produces the useable and sustainable up-to-date expertise.

These are among the issues that WIPO faces in its broader development role. For WIPO, dissemination also has a broader meaning beyond its crucial role in PCT processes and information provision. As we saw in Chapter 2, its core mandate is, in effect, threefold in nature:

- to enhance and expand the membership of states to the various existing IP conventions;
- to develop new and improved IP conventions and regimes;
- to offer technical assistance to developing countries.

All of this can seen as a form of dissemination in an overall sense and in fact it is a role that is expanded by obligations under the TRIPs agreement.

The EPO and several national offices are also engaged directly in assisting countries facing new demands for various forms of IP reform, in some cases starting from a virtual zero base. The EPO has a considerable development role among developing countries and among the former Communist regimes of Eastern Europe. The USPTO and CIPO are involved in assisting Mexico. And the USA and the AIPO are involved in the Asia Pacific in ensuring that viable intellectual property regimes are established, preferably at a regional level (AIPO, 1995).

IP dissemination II: a more aggressive value-added IP dissemination role?

As mentioned, there are some grounds for discussing, albeit briefly, a second IP dissemination role. It is not a role promoted or advocated by all jurisdictions but it has implications that are worth noting. At its root it is a role which suggests that, in principle, IP agencies or industry departments could be and should be much more aggressive suppliers (marketers? facilitators?) of the generation and distribution of value-added IP information. In some instances, the desire to move in this direction is undoubtedly accompanied by a concern that the agency or department concerned might not survive or would lose influence unless it could take on such new aggressive service-oriented roles. But such suggestions are always almost immediately accompanied by caveats and counterpressures regarding just how 'entrepreneurial' such agencies/departments could, should, or would be allowed to be.

An example of this line of thinking came from Canadian developments both within the Department of Industry and CIPO but it was manifest in other jurisdictions as well, such as Australia and the UK. Industry Canada, the federal government's lead micro economic department, was clearly shifting its philosophy and mandate, in line with developments traced in Chapter 3, towards playing a knowledge role rather than a spending and subsidising role in industrial policy (Doern, 1995a). In addition, there was a strong desire to begin to look at its business framework regulatory areas not just as protective rules but also as a source of new information for business. Thus data on bankruptcy trends, patterns of new incorporation of firms, and patents and other intellectual property could be supplied to business, it was felt, in new and useful ways. These and other related service aspects were also seen as being a logical outgrowth of thinking in the Canadian Intellectual Property Office (CIPO) and also in the Canadian Government's overall initiative on service delivery. The more embellished versions of the need for reinvented and more entrepreneurial government, including finding new sources of revenue, were also present in this climate of thinking. Computer and information system enthusiasts also added grist to this kind of mill because of the ability to manipulate data in new, fast, interesting and inexpensive ways. In many industry departments, these enthusiasms were also further linked to developments to produce one-stop shopping for government information about business and for business.

Other jurisdictions also saw these same combinations of argument and pressure. AIPO's reports and the UK Patent Office reveal similar kinds of thinking as do some reports of their parent industry departments. But both CIPO and the other agencies were immediately aware of what the counterarguments and pressures were. For example, the British Conservative Government had absolutely no sympathy for its Patent Office or its Department of Trade and Industry being themselves entrepreneurial public service agencies or being in competition with business.

Another counterpressure came from within and outside the IP agencies where key interests said simply that any spare resources should, at the margin, go towards supporting the basic IP protection function and to improving pendency performance. This pressure came, and continues to come from big business, the profession and from the IP agencies' own examiner cadre.

A second kind of accompanying argument was that IP agencies, if allowed, would simply not be very good at it. An agency geared to a culture of technical control and the protection function would not be good at being itself entrepreneurial or innovative in any real sense. Besides, the proffered IP and other business framework information has many legal and other constraints around its collection that totally or partially prohibit its unfettered dissemination or its repackaged dissemination.

The further line of argument and pressure was simply that if value-added IP information could be supplied, it was the private sector itself that would discover these possibilities and which would be far more nimble and inventive in identifying and profiting from such business opportunities. In brief, IP agencies should not be allowed to play such value-added roles, an argument made by the aggressive small business lobby, including the fast growing consulting and information industries.

Because of these immediate counterpressures it is certainly necessary to conclude in this book that this second role is not in the ascendency in the agencies examined. CIPO's development of such concepts stresses that, if feasible, it would be carried out only as a limited facilitating activity. Thus, for example, CIPO might develop new potential information products and make them known to business, that would then develop them.

The ultimate reason for keeping this kind of aggressive role on the institutional analytical agenda, however, is that IP interests as a whole, including the IP profession, may already be seeing some of the presence of what might be called rogue traders in IP-related information. The profession has always been concerned about unqualified people practising in its name and has asked IP agencies themselves to police these activities.

One of the key features of new information technologies, however, is that they have an almost immediate potential to break down definitions of who carries out what lines of business. If the business is seen simply as information or as helping out in brokering innovation, then the presence of new value-added (including incompetent) IP information is quite possible and all the more likely. The USA has seen these developments emerge more than anywhere else, in part because it has a more entrepreneurial economy to start with.

Thus the pressure for a more value-added IP dissemination activity is likely to come from the private sector itself, including small business. But this author would personally not rule out the potential for this coming from IP agencies themselves, especially if national offices become concerned about their own survival or if the general trend is the need for many national offices to specialise in dissemination roles and to provide information to small and medium-sized businesses. The need for national offices to rely on fees rather than tax dollars may also exert pressure over the long run to charge for basic information and to find new sources of information that could be charged for. This is happening in many countries in respect of other government agencies which have similar information roles (e.g. statistical agencies, geological survey agencies).

IP dissemination III: new users and the fostering of an IP and innovation-oriented economic culture

The IP Dissemination III role refers not necessarily to the stock of IP information but rather to getting information out about the IP regime as a whole to firms and inventors which do not yet use it. In one sense this also is a role which IP agencies have informally been carrying out for some time, but the difference now is that it is frequently linked to a more explicit goal of fostering a greater IP culture or an innovation culture in the national (and global) economy.

Perhaps the best place to locate the issues involved in this third area of IP dissemination is to examine the main features of a 1994 study by the EPO (European Patent Office, 1994). It examined the utilisation of patent protection in Europe. The context for the study and for the EPO's concerns was centred on Europe's relative declining patent usage compared to the USA and Japan. For example, the study showed that between 1987 and 1993 first filings in the USA had risen by 47 percent from 68,000 to 100,000 (European Patent Office, 1994, p. xi). In Japan, where strict comparison is more difficult, first filings had increased from 310,000 to 332,000 in the same period, despite a policy in Japan to encourage the filing of *fewer* patents (European Patent Office, 1994, p. xi). This latter, seemingly curious policy was launched because of the tendency of Japanese industry to patent almost anything, often tactically, at prematurely early stages of thought and invention.

In contrast, patent usage in Europe had stayed constant at about 89,000 for several years after a period of growth in the early to mid-1980s. As a further indicator of IP usage, the study noted that if data on first filings per million inhabitants were compared, Japan stood at 2665, the USA at 388, and Europe at 245 (European Patent Office, 1994, p. xii). The study also showed that European patents were mainly in traditional technologies with stagnating markets and were not growing in the newer areas such as biotechnology and computers and information sciences.

The EPO study sought on this basis to identify information about actual and potential patent applicants among the production industries of Europe. The EPO agenda was also strongly motivated by the desire to seize the potential of small and medium-sized enterprises (SMEs) since they were seen as a crucial link in the overall innovation chain or set of dynamics.

The EPO study concluded that 'the target group for patent activities in Europe is relatively small' perhaps only 3 percent of 13 million companies (European Patent

Office, 1994, p. 17). Only 16 percent of these approximately 360,000 companies had already filed patents at the national, European or international levels. The study also found wide variations in patent usage and potential among European states, strongly correlated with their overall level of economic development.

Among the other conclusions drawn in the EPO study were the following:

- 'The large group of non-applicants ... has (so far) banked mainly on secrecy for securing their competitive advantage and thus would have to be convinced of the advantages of protection.
- 'As non-applicants in particular put a higher premium on quality and service aspects than on patents as a comparative tool, SMEs ... must first be made aware of this essential means of protecting innovation.
- 'In comparison with Japan ... SMEs (in Europe) are more cautious in accessing the inventive value of their developments and are more reticent when it comes to filing patents. This leads us to conclude that access to patents should be made easier, especially for SMEs, so that the length of the procedure or its cost cease to be the determining factors in any decision whether or not to file.
- 'The fact that the commercial utilization of patented inventions is relatively high among (European) SMEs ... show that – unlike in Japan – fewer patents are filed for purely strategic reasons (e.g. in order to control a product market). As markets become increasingly global European SMEs will certainly have to place greater emphasis on integrating strategic aspects more closely into their innovation and patent policy.
- 'There is generally a serious lack of awareness of patent protection procedures among non-applicants, so companies (especially small and medium-sized ones) in the relevant sectors need to be approached direct.
- 'As a source of information on technical developments non-applicants in particular rate patent documentation well behind talks with customers, specialized literature, trade fairs and technical research (European Patent Office, 1994, p. 17).

These conclusions are European centred but the issues they raise and reflect can be found in each of the jurisdictions being examined.

Consider first the issue of how a given country sees itself in the IP/innovation 'league tables'. It is precisely such league tables that are, in a sense, replacing or supplementing the old comparative league tables which tended to be centred on what percentage of GNP a country spent on R&D (Nelson, 1993). But what, one might ask, does one make of either criterion? Canada for example, can easily see itself as a mini-Europe in this regard since its citizens and firms have not been aggressive or active patent filers. Indeed, as recently as the mid-1980s, the MacDonald Commission on the Canadian economy was warning Canadians that they must abandon their historic reliance on natural resource-driven growth (hewers of wood and drawers of water) and rely more on their wits (to interpret this read IP and innovation). Australia has had similar views expressed about its economy. Mexico, and several of the southern European countries face their own even more severe versions of these IP/innovation league table pressures and how to respond positively and practically to them.

Consider next the issue of small and medium-sized enterprises. The institutional issues here are dual in nature. First, there is the issue of both reaching and mobilising this subset of firms as an interest group. Second, there is the issue of reaching the firms as quite literally single enterprises or customers of an IP agency. The dual SME focus is partly a natural and logical one. They are indeed an important engine and source of innovation. SMEs are also a vital political phenomenon in that national small business lobbies have formed in most jurisdictions. This is especially true in the USA and Canada. It has been a bottom-up, almost populist lobby that has led the criticism against government regulation, redtape and a host of micro-economic policy and governance issues. The small business lobby, however, is also geared to a considerable criticism of big business as well, especially the major banks but also other areas of big business that have excessively privileged relations with government. The small business lobby is implicitly very interested and concerned about innovation but, as the EPO study conclusions indicate, it often does not speak directly about IP or patents. It sees many items related to its potential capacity to be innovative and these vary on a firm-by-firm basis. And it wants services that are inexpensive and efficient.

It is at this point in the analysis that one must reintroduce converging developments that we have already referred to earlier and in previous chapters about parent industry departments and their views about what modern competitiveness policies are or have become. This means recalling that the tariff and the use of major subsidies are increasingly less available to national industry departments because of trade rules, a lack of money and a sense that they did not work all that well in any event. Industry departments are accordingly all, albeit in varying degrees, transforming themselves into ministries that are relying more on:

- the provision of knowledge and information for business;
- a focus on SMEs as the main target group for such knowledge and service delivery;
- the use of trade policy instruments and negotiations to secure international access and protection for business in general but especially for their larger firms.

These points suggest that SMEs and industry ministries have been gradually reaching out to find and embrace one another but the rub is knowing in practical terms what each wants out of the marriage or partnership. Innovation is increasingly seen as a multifaceted multiservice-based, network-like series of relations within firms, among firms, between firms and government, within government, and among knowledge institutions such as universities and technical professions (Nelson, 1993; CIPO, 1994; 1994a). IP is but one feature of such a web of activities and relationships, and patents, trademarks, copyright, and integrated circuits are in turn, still further subsets of activity.

Because the needs vary, at the firm level one has to reach individual firms about their actual or potential use of IP but always in relation to other needs as well. However, because IP dissemination roles are the secondary not the dominant operating impulse of IP institutions, an SME-oriented collective interest group constituency must be mobilised if more emphasis is to be put on this activity. The latter is therefore a political problem because the small business lobby must be mobilised so that pressure can be put on IP agencies to start serving their needs, which are in the short term information oriented but which in the longer term will help, it is hoped, produce more patent-filing firms.

Because innovation-oriented government-based services to business are densely interconnected, a logical question arises. Should IP agencies deliver these IP services? They clearly have the IP expertise but not the other innovation-related expertise. Should it be one-stop business service branches in the larger industry department? They could mobilise the broader array of expertise and would know more about the microeconomy as a whole but they would lack the IP expertise.

Similar problems of coordinative capacities and ranges of relevant expertise occur if one thinks of dissemination in a private sector context. Consider first the IP profession in this regard. Within its core relationship with IP clients, IP professionals frequently find themselves advising on related innovation matters or in putting their clients in touch with the right expertise. But the IP profession is very cautious about seeing itself as playing an expanded role in these areas. It sees itself, as Chapter 4 showed, mainly in terms of the IP protection function. It is also very reluctant, indeed opposed, to the IP agency devoting too many agency resources to IP Dissemination II or III, if it is at the expense of the protection function.

The other actual and potential private sector supplier of these linked innovation/ IP services are private consulting, venture capital, and computer information firms. As mentioned in the previous section, these firms are growing in number but do not necessarily possess the requisite expertise. This is, of course, precisely where Adam Smith-like arguments will and should be mounted. In brief, markets are good coordinators and firms, including SMEs, will find one another and one another's relevant useful services and innovation needs.

A further element of the IP/innovation nexus must also be mentioned since the nexus increasingly goes beyond SMEs and big business and extends to universities and research and innovation institutes of various kinds. This line of thinking about innovation has spawned a view that industrial policy must be highly decentralised, urban and/or high-tech region centred, and based on networking and partnerships of myriad kinds (Paquet and Roy, 1995; Roy, 1995). This view evokes the development of Silicon Valleys, the Italian regions, and the Kitchener-Waterloo centres of reinforcing and interacting innovation activities and influences.

For universities and institutes, these and other kinds of developments force the need for institutions to think about how they will interact with their communities and also what policies they have, or do not have, about intellectual property. Universities, for example, are institutionally disposed to the free exchange of information and knowledge. But they are also increasingly involved in joint research with business where issues of patents are involved. Universities are also under pressure to raise their own revenues. In these and other respects, IP Dissemination III means not just IP building but institution building as well in the sense of having the right policies and incentives in place.

It is in the context of this cluster of ideas, pressures and practical service delivery problems that each of the six agencies is seeking to expand its IP Dissemination III roles. A sample of their practices and problems is instructive in this regard.

The UK Patent Office's focus has been on a number of initiatives. These include:

- an Open Days initiative held in Newport, Wales, for customers and contacts around the UK;
- a four-part interactive training package 'Making it Happen' aimed increasingly at tertiary education and the large company sector;
- the Roadshow programme which toured the country and was aimed at SMEs (UK Patent Office, 1994, item 5).

All national patent offices face similar dilemmas in the mounting of these services. The first is obtaining funding for them. The second is in evaluating them. For example, it is difficult to know whether any observed increases in patent filings is due to the new services or is caused by some other set of factors. In the case of these UK initiatives, it is, of course, possible that the services might generate new business for the EPO rather than for the UK Patent Office, although this would still be good for the UK and Europe.

In Australia, AIPO's efforts at increasing awareness of industrial property is also multifaceted. It is linked to a desire to get a better balance of services among its many stakeholders and to related services such as those of BizHelp and the Business Network Program (Australian Industrial Property Organization, 1995, p. 7). It is certainly appropriate as well to link these concerns to the previously discussed Australian report on petty patents, which, as Chapter 4 showed, was championed by small business interests.

At the international level, the dissemination issues become even more complex. For example, the EPO participates in a series of trade fairs in different member countries to enhance IP awareness and, of course, to help remedy the situation identified in the EPO study mentioned earlier. Thus the EPO is engaged, but it must also be cautious in these activities precisely because of national sensitivities. The EPO cannot just walk into any country and run an awareness programme. The national IP office, especially if it is only a dissemination office, will often want this function as its own. And, besides, national offices are far more likely to know national SMEs than is a Munich-based agency. Moreover, the European Union's concerns about the principle of subsidiarity is a further decentralist pressure.

For WIPO, the dissemination function is different again. It must preface the offer of its services on the basis that it will respond 'at the request of' individual governments or groups of developing or developed countries. But WIPO is engaged in many such invited activities. With respect to developing countries it has a somewhat broader and more active role. For example, this includes cooperative initiatives aimed at greater IP awareness among:

- secondary school students;
- higher educational institutions in management, engineering, science and technology;
- small and medium-sized enterprises;
- the general public (World Intellectual Property Office, 1995d).

Dispersed interests and the IP dissemination roles

The final aspect of the IP dissemination role is simply to appreciate in institutional terms that the interests that cluster around this role are indeed more numerous and dispersed, and therefore in part weaker politically. In short, it is harder for them to pressure IP agencies and industry departments and it is more difficult for IP agencies to reach out to them and identify their needs, and then to deliver appropriate services. Each of the IP agencies, as is evident even in the basic way they describe their 'stakeholders' and/or 'clients' and 'users', is seeking to broaden its links with these dispersed interests. Indeed these interests go beyond those which are so briefly noted in this final section of the chapter. For example, virtually all of the national agencies list their industry department and, crucially, their trade department as important clients, the latter because of the increasingly frequent policy changes being driven by trade agendas. For the two international IP bodies, EPO and WIPO, the key list of interests starts with member nation states and their IP agencies through whom, in turn, most national interest group demands are channelled. As we show later in this chapter, however, the EPO and WIPO also receive direct forms of lobbying.

In focusing here on a few summary illustrative examples of these dispersed interest/client relations, the point must be reemphasised that the relative exclusion of big business and the IP professions in this chapter should not be taken to mean that they have no stake in the IP dissemination role. They are, in fact, among the major users of such information and are a crucial political determinant of just how far IP dissemination roles will be allowed to evolve and grow.

The first interest/client relationship in this category is clearly small and medium-sized enterprises. The previous sections have already suggested the nature of the problems here. SMEs are a key client group for the expansion of IP awareness and for innovation. SME lobby groups vary in their degree of mobilisation. They are seemingly stronger in the USA, Canada and Australia, but perhaps less organised in the UK and Europe. In the USA, for example, SMEs have long ago secured a fee structure that offers lower fees for them compared to big business (USPTO, 1995). Second, where SMEs are organised, their policy agendas are far broader than IP and they see innovation as a seamless web of activities. Third, it is harder for such groups to mobilise at international levels. By definition, there are simply greater costs of lobbying and more compromises to make to reach consensus positions within whatever kind of loose membership vehicle might exist or might be assembled.

A second interest/client relationship is that between IP agencies and small inventors. This interest can, of course, overlap with the SME sector but the role of the small individual inventor is important. The individual as inventor is the ultimate mythical client and even raison d'être for patent regimes in some general populist sense. Mythical interests are always partially real, indeed vitally real. Many accounts of economic and social history give proper place to path-breaking inventions by individuals that created whole new industries (Diebold, 1990; Flatow, 1992).

Relative to other IP interests, this client is perhaps the most dispersed. Except for the USA and Japan, most national IP agencies search in vain for an organisation that might speak for this interest. However, such individual inventors can at times attract political attention by going to the media and/or by lobbying their elected representatives about the need the help the 'little person'. For example, in the UK a group of about 350 inventors exists called the Intellectual Property Development Confederation. Recently, it announced that it was seeking to obtain public funds from the UK Millennium Commission to fund an inventors' centre (*The Independent*, December

28, 1995, p. 4). One lead press editorial strongly backed the move in an editorial titled 'Backing the British Boffin', thus simultaneously backing innovation but also reinforcing the stereotype of the odd-ball inventor (*The Independent*, December 28, 1995, p. 12).

In the USA the individual inventor lobby is quite strong and has recently had two closely connected opportunities when its mobilising powers were shown to be vocal and effective (Hattenbach, 1995). The first was centred around the TRIPs agreement. The small inventor lobby saw the 20-year rule, in combination with the US implementating legislation, as being an attack on the small inventor. In particular, it argued that it would make it more difficult to obtain financing and venture capital (Hattenbach, 1995). This argument was linked to a view that the former US provisions guaranteed 17 years' protection whereas the TRIPs provisions provided for a maximum of 20 years but not necessarily a sufficient guarantee for bankers and financiers deciding to back a small inventor.

The second US example of the political pressures applied by this kind of IP lobby came in the Congressional battle over whether to convert the USPTO into an independent corporation. In general, small inventors opposed this move because they thought it would make the USPTO into a big business preserve and, by severing the taxpayer link, it would reduce their ability to appeal to populist thinking legislators (National Academy of Public Administration, 1995).

Partially overlapping these interests and partially going beyond them are players such as universities and various knowledge networks. Educational institutions, despite being big and potentially well-moneyed stakeholders, are also in many respects surprisingly hard to reach in IP dissemination or other matters. All the national offices bemoan the lack of operationally sustainable contact points. Some particularly aggressive individual universities (i.e. entrepreneurial universities) initiate their own contacts. For example, and perhaps somewhat surprisingly, the EPO often has more contact from a few US universities than it does from European ones. University interests of course extend potentially across a wide set of IP activities. They are potential greater patent holders than has thus far been the case but they are also ever broader users of IP information. All the agencies are seeking ways for universities to increase IP awareness in a host of science, engineering, law and business programmes. Universities also have important copyright concerns both through faculty who are authors and through students and libraries which are users of copyright material. Universities also have individual faculty who are themselves entrepreneurial and who apply pressure within the university to change rules or to recognise IP opportunities, but who are typically part of a minority in a traditional university culture that favours the dissemination and free exchange of information and ideas.

The brief mention of copyright matters should serve as a useful reminder that the interests being summarily profiled here tend to be seen in the context of patents. Suffice it to say that when one examines IP areas such as trademarks and copyright the cluster of interests both widens and deepens. The trademarks realm tends to bring in many more SMEs even than patents simply because many SMEs already have registered trademarks. And copyright brings in quite diverse groups from consumers of recordings and entertainment products through to producers, performers, broadcasters and the aforementioned educational institutions and libraries.

The most evident formal vehicles through which the IP agencies are striving to relate to these more dispersed and diverse interests is through advisory councils and through a greater and more regular use of surveys of user needs and user assessments of the quality of the services provided. In Australia, AIPO is advised by a recently established Advisory Council on Industrial Property (AIPO, 1995, p. 7). Canada and the UK have similar advisory groups with persons on them from some of the interest/client groups noted earlier, as well as the IP profession.

Perhaps the dilemmas of representation are best revealed in the two international bodies where nation states are the prime political representative. For example, user groups have pressed the EPO for direct representation on the EPO's governing Administrative Council but these pressures have been strongly resisted. When one moves further up the IP governance pyramid to a world body like the WIPO, the representational conundrum is stark. A quick sampling of WIPO documents shows a listing at the end of the dozens of non-governmental organisations which attend various WIPO meetings as observers or which take part in various WIPO sponsored conferences. One overall report noted 36 such groups including overarching international groups (in effect, a group of groups) such as the International Chamber of Commerce, the International Association for the Protection of Intellectual Property, the International Trademark Association, the Software Publishers Alliance, and the International Council of Archives, to name but a few (World Intellectual Property Organization, 1995c).

In the overall IP institutional milieu it is crucial then to see these sets of players as both interests and clients. In the former sense they may need to be mobilised or they are already groups with great influence. In the latter sense they need to be provided with services that are operationally effective but not at the level of interest groups. They must be served at the individual firm or organisational level as real users of IP. There is a difference, in short, between seeing them politically and serving them at a front-line operational level.

Conclusions

This chapter has shown that the IP dissemination function is, on the one hand, a central part of the IP trade-off but that it is, on the other hand, in many respects, a very secondary impulse in the inner operating culture of IP agencies. Nonetheless, the evidence across the agency jurisdictions clearly indicates that the IP agencies are seeking to expand or rebalance the IP dissemination role in comparison with the IP protection role. The transformation of the IP agencies into corporate or executive agencies has helped foster this effort.

The analysis indicates, however, that the IP dissemination roles are complex and that there is value in seeing in the late 1990s at least three kinds of role. The basic role of making use of the existing stock of IP information is a long and well-established one with business being the dominant users but with other users benefiting as well, including IP examiners, government in general, and universities and R&D centres.

The actual and potential emergence of IP Dissemination II has been discussed. It embraces the provision of a more aggressive value-added form of IP information either by IP agencies themselves and/or by private firms trading in the increasingly amorphous and boundary-breaking IP/innovation service sector of the economy. Some IP agencies want to play this role but there are strong political counterforces in and outside IP agencies which say that they should not and will not be allowed to compete with the private sector in these value-added markets.

The IP Dissemination III role has also been shown to be important as each jurisdiction seeks to reach out to new IP applicants and users, especially among SMEs but also among other sectors such as universities. This role, and IP dissemination activities in general, have been shown to be tied up in extremely important debates about just what innovation entails and hence, institutionally, into relations with industry departments and their service roles in the knowledge economy. These debates in turn raise important issues about which interests should pay for IP dissemination services.

In the dissemination function as a whole it is evident that IP agencies must deal with, and strive to reach, a much more dispersed set of interests than is encountered in the protection function where big business and the IP profession are dominant. The latter two interests have a big stake in the dissemination role, but the latter role inextricably involves more dispersed players and generally less organised stakeholders. These include SMEs, small individual inventors, universities and institutes. And internationally, the players extend ever more broadly as one involves the even larger needs of developing countries and the ever broader constituencies of players that seek to influence bodies such as EPO and WIPO.

CHAPTER SIX

Trademarks and IP Institutions

To the layperson, trademarks and the trademark regulatory and institutional process are in many ways the least known aspects of IP institutions. In most national IP offices trademarks constitute the second highest volume of applications and revenues but well behind those of patent applications. Trademarks arguably fall behind both patents and copyright when conceived of as IP or as 'creations of the mind'. Patents deal with products that are seen to be scientific and technical, in short what many see as 'real' inventions. Copyright evokes the creations of authors and musicians and, of course, has been the object of growing political attention within the IP field. Trademarks are the product of establishing recognised designations and marks and thus seem like a lower order of creativity. Somehow one does not want to put the golden arches of McDonald's in the same creative league as a Booker Prize-winning novel or the invention of the light bulb. But in the economics of creativity, trademarks are a crucial part of the innovation and commercial process to help differentiate and designate the quality and content of products and services.

Regardless of their implied secondary or tertiary status in the league rankings of IP, trademarks are an important aspect of IP institutions and IP law (Bainbridge, 1994; Cornish, 1996). The structure and behaviour of IP institutions cannot be fully understood without examining the key features of the trademark regulatory process. In this chapter, we look at it in four steps. First, we examine what trademarks are and what the nature of the protection versus dissemination functions are in this realm of IP. Second, we trace out the typical trademark registration process as it proceeds within an IP body. Third, we examine how the trademark business is situated in the operations of national and international IP bodies. Fourth, we look illustratively at how recent issues are affecting the structure of interests – business, consumers, and others in the trademark field. These centre on the development of the Internet and links between so-called domain names and trademarks, and on the way in which competition for the trademark profession is emerging out of the breakdown of boundaries in business and innovation services due to computerisation and Internet growth. Conclusions then follow.

Trademarks and the IP trade-off

If a trademark is 'any sign that individualizes the goods of a given enterprise and distinguishes them from the goods of its competitors' (WIPO, 1995, p. 191) then the nature of the IP trade-off between protection and dissemination is in many respects virtually simultaneous. The trademark protects the enterprise's individualised claim and simultaneously communicates something about the quality or nature of the goods it supplies to the market. Indeed, some may argue, that protection is far more dominant in trademarks compared to patents because there is no room for others to use the mark to, as it were, further innovation. However, there are important aspects of communication and advertising in the development and use of trademarks in that they inform consumers and reward businesses which produce high-quality goods.

While trademarks began literally centuries ago in the context of a goods-based economy, they also apply to services in the form of service marks. In the complex global economy the world of trademarks is also joined in some countries by a complex array of collective marks and certification marks. These indicate either the affiliation of enterprises that use the collective mark or the specified standards met by certification marks.

National IP laws vary in the definitions of these kinds of marks and also, to some degree in the kinds of signs which may serve as marks. Signs could be in the form of words, letters and numerals, devices, coloured marks, three-dimensional signs, sounds and even smells. But there are practical limits governed by the registration process, in that signs must be capable of being published in a trademark journal to inform the public and trademark holders of the registration or proposed registration.

The registration of trademarks (details follow) is accordingly seen within IP offices as being closer to an art itself when compared to, for example, the granting of patents which turns on science and technological judgement. This is because the crucial first requirement of registration is that the mark must be distinctive, a judgement that in part depends on how it is seen by consumers. But signs can be registered that are already in existence in the market or it can be a sign that has not been used before. Trademark regimes vary in the extent to which the burden of proof rests with the applicant or the registrar to show that distinctiveness is present. But lack of distinctiveness is the central ground on which an application can be refused. Lack of distinctiveness could be evidenced by such things as the use of generic terms (coffee, tables etc.) and certain kinds of geographical origin.

Marks may also be denied registration if they are deemed to be contrary to other public interest norms. These can include marks judged to be:

- deceptive;
- contrary to morality (e.g. obscene pictures);
- reserved for use by the state or public or international organisations.

Implicit in this discussion is the point that trademarks can be protected through either registration or use. Registration is the more dominant mode but there are provisions that, in a dispute between the first user of a trademark and a registered user, the first user is given priority. However, once a trademark has been registered there is an expectation in law that the trademark will be used, although initial grace periods are provided for. Unused trademarks are a barrier to the registration of new marks and make no economic sense in terms of functioning markets.

Two other aspects of trademarks are inherent in this sketch of key features and their inherently judgemental nature. First, within countries, a much wider range of small firms and business are likely to be involved in seeking trademark rights compared to patent rights. In this sense, trademarks are more 'local' IP. Second, they are for large firms, increasingly global and, as we see later, they are caught up in interesting problems as many kinds of firms seek to use the Internet as a part of their marketing and as a site for establishing identity and doing business.

The trademark application and registration process

As suggested, obtaining a registered trademark involves a much more judgemental and non-technical process than patents. In this section, we present a basic account of the typical cycle in the application and registration process (the Canadian process is our model here but clearly there are some differences among countries).

At the front end of the process, the IP agency advises anyone inquiring about registering a trademark to obtain the services of a qualified trademark agent. As with patents, a similar initial process of advice and discussion, and preliminary searching occurs between the agent and the client/applicant. Of crucial initial importance is that in some countries such as the USA and Canada, the trademark must be used in that country before it can be registered. Thus, there are many unregistered trademarks used in the marketplace. Again, to use the Canadian example, the registration of a trademark is not required. Protection is available though the common law. Nonetheless, case law has restricted the scope of protection for common law trademarks to national protection only. The registered trademark provides national recognition and thus *prima facie* evidence of proof of ownership.

Once an application has been filed along with the fee, the trademark examiners in the IP agency search the trademarks database and other publications to determine if any other trademarks come into conflict with the applicant's mark or if there are other bars to registration. If there is such conflict, the agency immediately advises the applicant. The examination then proceeds through a formal examination/ negotiation process as the examiner seeks to ensure compliance with the law and its regulations. All objections from the examiner must be met or overcome. Typically, however, this process is much shorter than for patents, in large part because the judgements needed are less technical.

If met, then a formal publication phase ensues in which the agency publishes the application in a trademarks journal, typically a weekly publication. Publication triggers a potential 'challenge process'. On payment of a fee, anyone, within a specified period of the date of publication, may file a statement of opposition with the IP agency. Challenges are reviewed, in a court-like adversarial process by a trademarks opposition board. Again, this is usually a board with delegated authority from the head or registrar since it is the latter, as a statutory person (in the Canadian case) who registers or denies the registration of a trademark. The whole challenge process can take a year, or two in some jurisdictions.

Following any challenge process, the parties are notified of the final decision and the reasons for it. If there is no opposition or if an opposition is decided in favour of the applicant, the application is then allowed. A notice of allowance or similar notification is sent to the applicant, and, upon payment of a further fee (and proof of use, in the Canadian case) the trademark is registered. If someone opposing the trademark is unsuccessful in the challenge process, there are avenues of appeal (in Canada to the Federal Court). As is the case with patents, the policing of trademark infringements (whether a trademark is registered or not) is a private legal matter by way of court injunction and/or damages.

Trademarks also have processes for the international filing and registration of marks. These flow from the 1891 Madrid Agreement Concerning the International Registration of Marks ('Madrid Agreement' (as revised)) and the Protocol Relating to the Madrid Agreement, which was adopted in 1989, entered into force on December 1, 1995 and became operational in April 1996 (World Intellectual Property Organization, 1995, Chapter 21; and 1997). The purpose of the Madrid Agreement is to provide for the international registration of trademarks. In essence, the process is to enable the applicant to comply with one set of formalities at WIPO by submitting an application in one language (French) with fees paid once to WIPO and with protection secured for 20 years in all countries in which protection has effect.

The international registration process begins in the country of origin. The national IP office checks that the mark is registered and then forwards the application to WIPO. A fee is paid to WIPO which covers a basic fee as well as a complementary fee for each country for which protection is requested. These fees are distributed between WIPO and the national offices. WIPO then completes the registration process in line with the Madrid Agreement and its regulations.

While this process has facilitated international registration, there are still problems, in part revealed by the delays in ratifying the Madrid Protocol. This 1989 protocol was to facilitate the accession of new member countries but key countries such as the USA and Japan have not agreed to join because of concerns about the overall agreement. The concerns centre on provisions that would allow international registrations to be based on national applications rather than national registrations. There are also concerns over the processes of refusals and oppositions as well as concerns about links with the emerging European Trademark (see later).

IP agencies and their core trademark business

The trademark business is typically the second line of operation for the agencies being examined in this book. It is second behind patents in the inherent prestige of the process and in the organisational culture of the agencies. It is second in its revenue-raising importance for the agency. But it may not be second in terms of its underlying political and client support for the IP agency in that trademark applications and interests are more numerous and broad in scope across the small to big business spectrum and across the sectors of the economy. Moreover, trademark applicants are far more likely to be from the country's own citizens and firms than are patent applicants, where foreign applicants may well be dominant, especially in smaller or medium-sized countries such as Canada or Australia.

While the second business-line status of trademarks is borne out by the information published by national IP offices, there are also indications that trademarks and trademark revenues have been growing at a faster rate of growth in recent years. The USPTO shows a steeper path of growth in trademarks and indicates that 'since 1989, the trademark application workload has increased approximately 87 percent', considerably more than for patents (USPTO, 1994, p. 10). Trademarks filed in fiscal year 1994 were alone up by 11 percent over the previous year. Trademarks were also closing the gap in revenue terms compared to patents. Trademark receipts for the USPTO grew from $125.2 million in 1992 to $155.4 million in 1994 compared to $172.5 million and $186.1 million for patents in the same period (USPTO, 1994, p. 2). The USPTO was also paying much more attention than previously to pendency rates for trademarks, not only because of this greater volume but also because of pressure from the business community and the IP profession.

There are similar tendencies in Canada and Australia. In Canada, CIPO's data show trademarks filed growing from 25,194 in 1993–94 to 29,528 two years later, whereas patents filed grew more slowly (CIPO, 1994, p. 15; 1995). In Australia, both patents and trademarks were growing at similar rates (AIPO, 1995, p. 18).

The situation in the UK was somewhat different in that trademarks filed in the early 1990s actually fell at the start of the 1991–92 recession and then in 1994 surpassed its late 1980s levels (UK Patent Office, 1994, p. 20). The UK situation on trademarks will undoubtedly now be increasingly affected by the functioning of the new European Trademark Office in Alicante (see later).

Regardless of whether trademarks have been recently growing or not, the national IP offices have all had to devote more energy and thought as to how to improve trademark pendency rates but the offices vary as to their willingness to commit themselves publically to service standards for faster pendency of the trademark application and registration process.

On the international front, the World Intellectual Property Organization (WIPO) sees itself as a facilitator and intermediary in the overall world trademark registration and commercial process mainly through the Madrid Agreement. Its latest publications highlight the fact that worldwide in 1995 there were about one million registrations and renewals of marks but that this number did not include the '22,660 international registrations and renewals under the Madrid Agreement which corresponds to some 226,000 national registrations or renewals' (WIPO, 1997, p. 9). Similarly, in 1995 WIPO points out that there were more than 8 million registrations of marks in force but that this figure also did not include '300,000 international registrations under the Madrid Agreement which corresponds to approximately 3 million national registrations' (WIPO, 1997, p. 9).

These data show the importance of international trademark registration but they also indicate their second place status in revenue terms. WIPO's own financial information shows that the Madrid system was budgeted for 1997 to supply just under 24.2 million Swiss francs of WIPO's almost 150,000 million income (WIPO, 1997, p. 96). Patents under the PCT registration system constituted almost 91 million Swiss francs (WIPO, 1997, p. 96). Trademark revenues are likely to grow absolutely and as a percentage of WIPO revenues in the next few years but this depends in part on how internationalised the trademark process is allowed to become. The more lucrative it becomes for WIPO, the more important the sharing of fees between WIPO and national offices may become as well.

WIPO also has important responsibilities in the trademark field, as in other IP mandate areas, to promote the development of appropriate overall IP laws and regimes in developing countries. Some of these issues are discussed in Chapter 8 since they are now clearly linked to the WTO and TRIPs. Of potentially greater importance in the coming years is WIPO's Arbitration and Mediation Centre. Established in 1994, it offers services for the resolution of international commercial disputes between private parties involving intellectual property (WIPO, 1997, p. 83). It is intended to administer a variety of dispute resolution procedures such as mediation, arbitration and expedited arbitration. It is too early to judge this aspect of WIPO's activities but it indicates a new kind of role that WIPO has been discussing and promoting with other interests such as the American Arbitration Association (WIPO, 1994) and the Swiss Arbitration Association (WIPO, 1995). As we see later in our discussion of domain names, this role especially may rise in importance in realms of private dispute between Internet domain names and trademarks.

Another important international institutional development in the trademark field is in Europe. The European Patent Office (EPO) has been in existence for some time but it has not had a role in trademarks (EPO, 1995; Doern, 1997). As we have seen, the EPO is an independent office and it is not an institution of the European Union. The development of a European trademark and designs system has only recently been given an institutional base. In this case, the institutions are centred in the European Union, namely in the Office for Harmonization in the Internal Market (OHIM) (Trade Marks and Designs). Located in Alicante, Spain, the OHIM only began its Community trademark functions in 1995.

Unlike the EPO, the office is established under European Community law and is supervised by the Community courts. Like the EPO, it must derive all of its revenue from registration and renewal fees. An application for a Community trademark may be filed in one of the official languages of the European Union. However, any post-registration proceedings must be in one of the five languages of the Office (Spanish, German, English, French and Italian). A more restricted number of languages was deemed necessary to reduce operational burdens and the level of fees.

This last point regarding Europe brings out an institutional aspect of trademark institutional politics that is not as obvious when discussion is focused on English-speaking countries such as the UK, USA, Australia and Canada. All IP regulation is influenced to some extent by language and the language of commerce, but it occurs to the greatest extent in trademarks and is brought to the fore in the geo-politics of Europe. WIPO faces similar pressures and realities which in turn get built into the cost and fee structures of the registration process.

Changing trademark issues and related institutional interests

As in all aspects of IP, trademarks face new institutional issues which are transforming a once fairly stable and seemingly serene and even closed regulatory world. Two such developments are discussed briefly, one centred on domain names on the Internet and the other centred on pressures on how governments treat trademark agents as part of the IP profession. Both are ultimately linked by the technological impacts of computers and information services but they are invariably tied also to new or emerging interests which are in some respects new to the IP regime and which have different views about where the IP trade-offs should be made and who should profit from them.

Internet domain names and trademarks

The first interesting example where changing trademark issues and interests emerge is that of domain names on the Internet. The Domain Name System (DNS) is a key feature of the Internet's operational structure. It is designed for locating machines on the Internet. Machine names are a series of textual fields representing a registration based on a hierarchy, with authority delegated from the registry above

(International Ad Hoc Committee, 1997). Thus the top-level domain (TLD) registries are one for each country and a small number which are international.

For most of the still young Internet era, this domain system was adequate. But the massive commercialisation of the Internet has necessitated an expanded system. A key feature of the existing domain system is that it is commercially attractive precisely because it has a 'human-friendly' quality to it. But the more commercially used it becomes, the more the system potentially runs into conflicts with intellectual property issues, in this case, especially trademark protection.

A further interwoven institutional issue is that the existing system is in most respects the product of work not by governmental authorities but by the International Ad Hoc Committee (IAHC). IAHC describes itself as 'an international multi-organizational effort for specifying and implementing policies and procedures relating to TLD' (International Ad Hoc Committee, 1997). It is accordingly a form of self-regulating body that is both a partner and a challenge for established IP authorities and interests.

IAHC membership consists of a broad range of legal, administrative, operations and technical 'constituencies'. Representatives come from organisations that develop Internet products and technologies, that sponsor TLD administration, and review and define relevant international legal matters. IAHC also describes itself as an entity that will operate in the style of an Internet standards 'design team'. It will operate by 'formulating criteria and procedures' at the same time 'seeking review, modification and consensus from the rest of the Internet community' (International Ad Hoc Committee, 1997). It sees itself as an international resource that will in its specification activities pay particular attention to the questions of 'fairness and functional stability' (International Ad Hoc Committee, 1997).

Many of the key issues about trademarks and domain names were discussed at a major consultative meeting convened by the World Intellectual Property Organization held at Geneva in late May, 1997 (WIPO, 1997a). WIPO's discussion document for the event went beyond the problems with the present scheme for allocating domain names to the key issues regarding their links to trademarks. The WIPO document begins with the point that 'domain names are by their nature trademark-like, and are often used to direct users to the home page of a company whose domain name is also its trademark' (WIPO, 1997a, p. 1). Trademark considerations, however, had in general not been taken into account in the allocation of domain names.

The WIPO document was itself a response to a February 1997 IAHC Final Report on how to change the domain system to accommodate the new demands made on it and WIPO was also a participant in that IAHC process. IAHC made several recommendations including seven new generic top-level domains for various types of business or activity (e.g. recreation and entertainment, information services, personal nomenclature). Registration would occur in future through any of up to 28 new registrars spread around the world. It also recommended that international dispute procedures for the resolution of conflicts relating to trademarks or other IP rights and Internet domain names be established, and that they be administered by the WIPO Arbitration and Mediation Centre.

Thus a key issue emphasised by WIPO was centred on the mechanisms for introducing trademark concerns at or before the time of registration of a domain name. Some of this discussion centred on the availability of a worldwide database of trademarks that could be searched. But such a database currently has serious limitations. WIPO noted that there were many interested parties that supported some form of pre-screening of domain names to test for conflicts with trademarks. It also stressed, however, that there was little or no support for establishing a type of 'trademark examination' for domain names which would be very time consuming and expensive. There were also problems in how to handle non-registered trademarks.

The WIPO discussion paper also examined whether IP rights in domain names *per se* could be established, separate from existing IP rights. Many difficulties were noted in this regard including the potential conflict between generic names which are domain names but which cannot usually be registered trademarks.

WIPO later issued a document on the idea of using its mediation and dispute resolution processes which cover only commercial disputes among private parties (WIPO, 1997b). This document discussed some of the issues involved but it also revealed some of the perceptions that some IAHC and Internet community participants had about WIPO and established IP authorities. WIPO itself acknowledged that it had been 'criticized as representing large trademark owners only' but defended its role by saying that 'nothing could be further from the truth' (WIPO, 1997b, p. 2) and that its member countries included trademark offices whose largest constituencies were small and medium-sized trademark owners.

The Geneva consultative meetings clearly indicated the new complexities and fault lines of trademark rules and interests. Some of these were summarised by the chairman's review of the discussion (WIPO, 1997c). First, it was agreed that governance of the Internet was outside the scope of the meeting but that IP rights had to be fully protected on the Internet. Second, it indicated that the database idea for registered trademarks was important but needed further study and analysis. Third, there was support for the idea of dispute resolution and mediation but again considerably more work would need to be done regarding exactly how this could be achieved. Fourth, there was a consensus that the idea of a separate IP rights system in domain names should not be studied at this time.

Again, global differences are bound to arise in this realm of IP regulation. The USPTO, for example, has clearly indicated its policy in the USA that 'Internet domain names must meet the same requirements for registration as all trademarks and service marks' (US Patent and Trademark Office, 1998).

Trademark agents, the IP profession and competition

A second more subtle example of change regarding the dynamics of trademark processes and institutions is centred on the role of trademark agents in national and international IP agencies. A key feature of the trademark institutional dynamics of national and international IP agencies is the situation regarding the trademark agent in the larger IP profession and the pressures they are under compared to the more dominant patent lawyers or agents. These issues are in turn linked to the kind of professional background required and on the nature of inherent competition in the provision of these services in a computerised information economy.

As we have seen from the earlier description of the trademark application process, IP offices typically advise potential applicants to obtain the services of a qualified trademark professional. But the situation here is different from that which applies to patents, a fact borne out by the 1996 Australian study of its patent professions and how they are regulated (Australia, 1996). The Australian study pointed to four key differences (Australia, 1996, pp. 55).

1   The scientific or engineering education deemed to be essential to prepare patent applications 'is not a necessary prerequisite for a person engaged in the registration of trademarks'.
2   In trademarks, the high level of professional competence centres more in designing and reporting searches.
3   There is more scope in trademarks to correct initial errors whereas in patents an error in patent filing can 'result in the total loss of a valuable property right' (Australia, 1996, p. 55).
4   Self-filing of trademark applications is much more common (40 percent in Australia) and this itself indicates that individuals do not feel the same need for the advice of IP professionals.

When these features of the trademark regime were placed against the Australian Trade Marks Act 1995 which restricts who may work as a trademark agent, the Australian study reached the conclusion that competition in such services would be further aided by allowing others such as accounting and management consultants to provide trademark services. Indeed, it sought to allow 'any person to prepare and lodge trademark applications for gain' (Australia, 1996, p. 56).

There are in effect two kinds of institutional-economic pressures and developments that make trademark professionals more vulnerable. The first is found in the earlier reference to management consultants and to a fast growing set of information service firms. One of the key features of new information technologies, however, is that they have the potential almost immediately to break down definitions of who carries out what lines of business. If the business is seen simply as information or as helping out in brokering innovation, then the presence of new value-added (including incompetent) IP information and services is quite possible and all the more likely. The USA has seen these developments emerge more than anywhere else, in part because it has a more entrepreneurial economy to start with. But all countries are seeing more of the presence of what some in the IP profession might regard as rogue traders in IP-related information. The profession has always been concerned about unqualified people practising in its name and has asked IP agencies themselves to police these activities. But others, as in the case of the Australian study, might see these same developments as competition and innovation-promoting developments.

The second development concerning the vulnerability of trademark professionals occurs within their established professions and IP agencies. Because the trademark agent's set of skills comes closer to being a judgemental art rather than an activity involving science and technology, the trademark profession sees itself as being in the second rung within the larger IP profession. Patent agents or patent attorneys (depending on a country's designation) simply have more power within the profession either directly or in the context of the powerful mainstream profession of lawyers.

There is also a rapid globalising of the trademark lobby occurring in part due to its broader array of interests and its eclectic occupational base. This can be illustrated through a brief reference to the International Trademark Association (INTA). INTA is a leading lobby in the trademark field. It was formerly the United States Trademark Association and as such its roots go back to 1878 (International Trademark Association, 1997). Renamed as INTA in 1993, the organisation seeks to promote trademarks as an essential feature of world commerce. It lobbies national and international IP bodies on public policy matters and engages in educational activities aimed at businesses, the media and the public on the proper use of trademarks. Its membership includes more than 3200 firms and corporations in 117 countries (International Trademark Association, 1997). These include both small and large firms in a wide range of industries, including financial services, electronics, aerospace, consumer goods and textiles. Membership also includes other businesses that advise trademark owners such as the IP professions, advertising agencies, design firms and other industry associations.

Conclusions

This chapter has shown that trademarks are the second line of business for most IP agencies ranking behind the core patent business both in the volume of business and revenues they generate and in the inherent prestige of the activity within the agency's organisational culture. The nature of the trademark application and approval process also sets it apart from patents in that, at its core, it is closer to an art than to a science and technology-centred process of judgements and decisions. This feature is also central to why trademark examiners within IP agencies and trademark agents in the larger IP profession have a greater struggle for recognition and inherent status than their patent-based colleagues.

The trademark aspects of IP regimes are also characterised by a somewhat lesser developed set of internationalised processes compared to patents. This is partly due to the considerable importance of the language of commerce which seems to be greater in trademark matters. But it is also due to the fact that trademarks can exist without being registered. Moreover, the trademark process is influenced by a wider array of industrial sectors and ranges of small and large firms than is the case with patents and thus makes them more of a national and even local matter for firms who might never patent but who could be involved in trademarks as a part of their more basic marketing activities.

The chapter has also drawn attention to two examples of change which suggest that trademarks may be unusually susceptible to turbulence in the age of the Internet and of the telecommunications and digital revolution. Thus the discussion about domain names suggests that there are looming conflicts between trademarks and the central ways in which the Internet is managed. These conflicts are not just a function of how to manage it in a narrow sense but also because the Internet brings into play an array of interests, indeed 'networks of networks' of interests, who are much more likely than existing IP bodies to see the need for less rule-ridden and bureaucratic processes.

A smaller version of some of these same characteristics was revealed in the discussion about how the trademark profession was being viewed and challenged by related professions where the boundaries of information processing and related services increasingly blur. This means that many such providers can actually or potentially compete in the provision of advice to present and future trademark applicants and holders.

CHAPTER SEVEN

Copyright Regulatory Institutions

Our focus now shifts to copyright regulatory institutions but in a way that is initially quite different from our treatment of patents and trademarks. First, unlike trademarks which are coupled with patents in the core regulatory business of IP agencies, copyright institutions are often not a part of the same agency. This is because copyright in most countries does not involve a registration process and its core institutions are more diffuse or pluralistic, extending within the state to cultural departments and beyond the state to a wider array of 'collective associations' or organisations of authors and performers. These differences must be appreciated if one is to understand IP institutions writ large. Second, our interest in copyright institutions is different because it is the international politics of copyright, coupled with the onslaught of digital technology, that is most driving and energising the overall IP agenda. This is important in its own right but it is also of interest in this book because it affects the political-economic environment of core IP agencies. In brief, there is only so much room for political attention and resources to be given to IP and in the 1990s copyright may be affecting patent and trademark-centred IP agencies through that fact alone.

Accordingly, in this chapter we need to develop a basic appreciation of copyright institutions but certainly not a detailed one (Rose, 1993). The analysis is organised into three parts. First, we describe the basic international treaties that have governed copyright and which served as the backdrop to the more turbulent trade-related copyright changes of the last decade. Second, we set out some of the basic or common features of national copyright regimes, including the greater pluralism and density of the interest group structure in that regime, especially compared to patents. This is followed in the third section by a discussion of some of the copyright institutional issues emerging from digitalisation and the governance of the information highway. We have already examined one aspect of this, namely domain names, with regard to trademarks and thus a complementary look is needed for some key copyright issues. Conclusions then follow.

Basic international protection

International protection of copyright dates back to 1886 when initially ten countries signed the Berne Convention for the Protection of Literary and Artistic Works. Presently 125 states are signatories (WIPO, 1997, p. 60). The Berne Convention was, in essence, the main international touchstone for copyright protection until the WTO–TRIPs agreement of 1994, which brought copyright and other IP issues more under the rubric of trade law. We discuss the WTO and TRIPs in Chapter 8 but the prior Berne Convention is an important underpinning to the overall copyright regulatory system.

Amended several times, the Berne Convention is centred on three principles and also contains provisions which define the minimum protection to be given to creators of works. There are also special provisions for developing countries if they wish to take advantage of them. The first principle in the Berne Convention is that of *national treatment* whereby works originating in one contracting state are given the same protection in each other contracting state as the latter grants to the works of its own nationals. The second principle is that such protection must not be conditional upon *compliance with any formality*. The third principle is that such protection is *independent of the existence of protection* in the country of origin. The minimum standards of protection deal with the specific works and rights that are to be protected and the duration. The works are defined broadly and the rights include those such as the right to translate, to make adaptations, to perform in public, etc. The duration, with some exceptions, is for 50 years after the author's death.

A second important international treaty is the Rome Convention for the Protection of Performers, Producers of Phonograms and Broadcasting Organizations. A much smaller number of states, currently 55, are a party to the Rome Convention whose focus is not on authors but on performers and related neighbouring rights. Unlike the Berne Convention which is administered through WIPO, the Rome Convention is administered jointly by WIPO, the International Labour Organization (ILO), and UNESCO (WIPO, 1997, p. 73). One of the interesting features about copyright regimes is that historically there was an international regime before there were very many national regimes. Most international regimes follow on from national laws but in the case of copyright the reverse has been true. The Rome Convention of 1961 was the later centrepiece of this effort at regime building. For example, neighbouring rights were a part of the Rome Convention but came only much later in many countries.

These two conventions have been joined, as Chapter 8 examines more fully, by the WTO–TRIPs agreement but there are also other treaties as different sets of countries push for, and join, other particular advances or extensions of international copyright law. One of these is the WIPO Copyright Treaty of 1996 (concluded but not yet in force). It extends the subject matter protected by copyright to computer programs and original compilations of data and other material (databases) which by reason of the selection or arrangement of their contents constitute intellectual creations (WIPO, 1997, p. 65).

International copyright treaties have become complex and varied as to their signatories and coverage, but clearly reveal a need to amend copyright as new technologies emerged. We return to this theme later in the chapter since it affects current views about copyright and related IP institutions in the era of the Internet and information highway (Jaszi, 1992; Burk, 1994; Aoki, 1996).

Key features of copyright regimes

Copyright regimes thus have a long history in international terms and in domestic laws and practices (Clark, 1960). But at their core is the desire to protect the rights of those who create artistic works, be they in the form of books, paintings, poems, sound recordings, films or other media of communications. What is protected by copyright law and institutions is 'creativity in the choice and arrangement of words, musical notes, colours, shapes and so on' and protection against those who copy such creations (WIPO, 1995, p. 159). Such protection, however, has some limits. Copyright begins with the creation of the work and typically extends for the life of the author and not less than 50 years after the death of the author. Of increasing importance in copyright regimes is the protection of rights which are related to or 'neighbouring on' copyright. Such neighbouring rights are typically of three kinds:

- the rights of performing artists in their performances;
- the rights of broadcasting organisations in their communications signals;
- the rights of producers of phonograms in their sound recordings.

Of crucial importance is the principle that copyright does not protect the ideas that underlie such creations but only the mode of expressing such ideas. The protection aspects of copyright regimes are also influenced by ideas that original authors of works have 'moral rights' as well as economic or property rights. Both rights typically exist in law. Moral rights as set out in the Berne Convention require member states to grant to authors a dual right:

- the right to claim authorship;
- the 'right to object to any distortion, mutilation or other modification of, or other derogatory action in relation to, the work which would be prejudicial to the author's honour or reputation' (WIPO, 1995, p. 165).

Moreover, such moral rights are seen as remaining with the author even after the author has transferred his or her economic rights.

However, international global regimes are still influenced by differences in emphasis. For example, France and other countries with a civil law tradition (see later) have been strong supporters of giving regimes an emphasis on moral rights whereas countries such as the USA, Canada, Australia and the UK which have common law traditions stress economic rights. Thus the civil law tradition tends to regard author's rights 'as natural human rights, or part of one's right of personality' (Keplinger, 1995, p. 15) and, hence, rights which cannot be waived. Economic rights, in many ways, are subordinated to moral rights. The implication also is that 'only works which are original, in that they reflect the personality of the author, are entitled to protection' (Keplinger, 1995, p. 15). A system of 'related rights' protects productions that do not meet this originality test.

Such an emphasis can also be seen at a more general level in discussions about European copyright policy. A 1995 EU Commission Green Paper stressed the importance of copyright and the new information industries in terms of extending the EU's internal market but linked copyright simultaneously with the vital 'cultural dimension' (Commission of the European Communities, 1995, p. 11). Thus the Green Paper saw copyright as being increasingly fundamental for 'the improvement of knowledge and dissemination of the cultures and histories of the European peoples, the promotion of cultural exchanges and of artistic creativity, and recognition of the value of the common cultural heritage' (Commission of the European Communities, 1995, p. 11). These cultural links and the broad issues of collective versus individual authorship have been examined extensively (Woodmansee and Jaszi, 1994).

In common law or Anglo-American legal systems the focus of the copyright regime is to promote 'the creation of works for the general public benefit by protecting the author's economic rights' (Keplinger, 1995, p. 14). A recent US study, also linking copyright to the Internet, reiterated the US view of copyright by citing a major US Supreme Court ruling. In it the court said that 'the primary purpose of copyright is not to reward the labour of authors, but "to promote the Progress of Science and useful Arts"', the latter phrase drawn from the US Constitution (US Information Infrastructure Task Force, 1995, p. 20).

The dissemination part of the copyright IP trade-off is that in the first instance, by supplying such protection, creativity will be stimulated and the results will be disseminated widely. In part, this is because copyright protects the author's original expression but encourages others to 'build freely upon the ideas and information conveyed by the work' (quoted in US Information Infrastructure Task Force, 1995, p. 20). This aspect of dissemination clearly has a private market aspect but the creativity may be disseminated in other ways as well. The US emphasis and language does not draw attention to overall cultural purposes as such but rather the public interest value of the 'useful' arts. This view has a more contemporary ring to it as well in the American tendency to regard its dominant and aggressive movie and entertainment industry as just that – entertainment – and not culture.

However, since globally, artistic works are seen firmly as part of a country's or people's cultural heritage, copyright and its protection/dissemination trade-off are linked to cultural policy in an overt way. Such norms extend in many developing and developed countries to the need to protect and disseminate traditional folklore. WIPO has had to address such issues particularly because several developing countries saw folklore as a key part of their cultural identity. Starting in the late 1960s several developing countries began to include provisions in their copyright laws to protect folklore (WIPO, 1995, p. 179). In industrialised countries expressions of folklore were considered to be in the public domain but others saw the issue differently (Aoki, 1996; Drahos, 1997). Accordingly, protection under copyright in some countries sought to protect against improper utilisation of expressions of folklore, 'including the general practice of making profit by commercially exploiting such expressions outside their originating communities without any recompense to such communities' (WIPO, 1995, p. 179).

Unlike patents and trademarks, there is in most countries no registration process for copyright (in the USA, however, there is a requirement to deposit a copy of published works in the Library of Congress). Originality must be present but there is no process for passing 'a test of imaginativeness, of inventiveness' or other sense of quality (WIPO, 1995, p. 161). Most national copyright laws protect the following works: literary, musical, artistic, maps and technical drawings, photographic, motion pictures and computer programs.

If the rights of a copyright owner are infringed through the unauthorised copying of materials for commercial purposes, the activity is referred to as piracy. Such piracy has always been a part of commerce but the extent and nature has changed greatly in recent years because of the telecommunications revolution. For example, Philips Electronics has announced that a new CD recorder is to go on the market which allows people to record their compact discs as easily as they can cassette tapes (*The Independent*, June 26, 1997, p. 3). The immediate reaction of the phonographic industry is that this development would greatly increase piracy and result in lost revenues and profits for the copyright holders.

The remedies for those whose rights have been infringed are typically based on civil redress. Injunctions are sought through the courts to restrain the continuation of the infringement and damages are sought. Debate about the efficacy of such compliance and enforcement aspects of copyright regimes have centred not only on international piracy but also on the speed of national remedies and the need for preliminary remedies before it is commercially too late for the copyright holder. The issue of copyright enforcement in an international context is a large and complex subject. We deal with it again in Chapter 8 because such enforcement issues were crucial to the WTO and TRIPs process and are best discussed there.

However, it is also important to appreciate how difficult it is within national systems. For example, in Canada and the USA, there have been strong protests from universities and other educational institutions which objected to new legislative provisions which would subject them to damages for unauthorised copying and which required them to keep track of copying to ensure adherence to the law. Prior to such changes, copying was seen as a virtual free public good under the concept of 'fair use'. The new collective associations that were strengthened under copyright reforms had little sympathy that their members should subsidise universities through illegal copying. Clearly, in examples such as this the tentacles of national enforcement have been extended in a very major way.

As mentioned earlier, a further crucial feature of copyright regimes is that the system needs an elaborate system of self-regulation and collective administration by creators. Workable institutions are needed to enable authors and creators to collect and distribute authors' fees. Authors and creators are typically small and numerous and face users who tend to be larger and more powerful. Moreover, the sites or venues in which creations might be sold or performed can be numerous. A composer for example, would find it literally impossible to know how often his country's hundreds of radio or television stations may have used his or her work. Thus collective administrative organisations are crucial both for authors and publishers and broadcasters (Smith, 1984; WIPO, 1995, Chapter 30). For example, the core role of an authors' organisation or society is to collect copyright fees and distribute the amount to the copyright owners, minus legitimate expenses but without the society itself making a profit. Beyond this core activity, the society typically performs a variety of functions, including: authorising the use of works of their members, checking on utilisation of their works; preparing model contracts; and offering advice and services (WIPO, 1995, p. 542).

In addition, other state-run institutions must serve linkage functions in the setting and implementation of fees and royalties. For example, in Canada, the Canadian Copyright Board has taken on broader functions as Canadian copyright law (propelled largely by trade commitments) has been changed. The Copyright Board was established in 1989 as the successor to the Copyright Appeal Board, itself created in 1936. The Copyright Appeal Board functioned as an administrative body to regulate the rates that collectives could charge for the use of the works contained in their repertoires. While the new Copyright Board assumed this role, its mandate was expanded to comprise five key areas of jurisdiction, namely to:

- establish tariffs for the retransmission of distant television and radio signals;
- establish tariffs for the public performance of music;

- adjudicate rate disputes between licensing bodies representing classes of copyright owners and users of their works;
- rule on applications for non-exclusive licenses to use published works of unlocatable copyright owners;
- set compensation, under certain circumstances, for formerly unprotected acts in countries that later joined the Berne Convention, the Universal Copyright Convention or the Agreement establishing the World Trade Organization (Copyright Board Canada 1996, p. 5).

Under a 1997 amendment, the mandate of the Copyright Board has been broadened and further augmented. Thus it will now establish tariffs with respect to neighbouring rights and takes on other specific responsibilities inherent in the stronger definition of creator rights. For example, with respect to educational institutions, the Board is empowered to adopt regulations prescribing the information to be kept in relation to the making, destruction, performance and marking of copies made, as well as the information to be sent to the collective societies involved (Copyright Board Canada, 1996a, pp. 3–4; Hébert, 1997, pp. 44–55).

Copyright, technological change and the information highway

Copyright law and institutions have always had to respond to new technologies from the printing press to movies to CD-ROMs. And so a key question in the late 1990s is whether the information highway and digital technology is qualitatively different from past technological changes and thus creates special institutional demands.

Consider first a smaller scale example of new pressures involving copyright and the telecommunications revolution. In 1996 a dispute arose between freelance writers and publishers in Canada over electronic copyright issues (*Globe and Mail*, May 22, 1996, p. A10). The Periodical Writers Association of Canada went before the Canadian Radio-television and Telecommunications Commission (CRTC) which was holding hearings into licence applications for new specialty TV channels. Among the applicants for licences were three major Canadian publishers. The freelance writers were arguing that the publishers were violating the copyrights of freelance writers, photographers and illustrators by repackaging and reselling their works without their permission and without recompense. The freelance writers were urging the CRTC, the telecomm regulator, to make copyright protection a condition of the licence of any new channel licences that might be awarded (*Globe and Mail*, May 22, 1996, p. A10). Other spokespersons also pointed to the French model where creators registered their works with their collective association. If anyone else wanted to make further use of it they would have to negotiate with the association and there were heavy fines if this was not done (*Globe and Mail*, May 22, 1996, p. A10).

The details of this episode are less important than some of its broad features. First, new converging technologies were involved. Second, a diffuse creator interest was taking on large concentrated user interests. Third, the creator group was in the midst of establishing a larger 'creators consortium' so that there was strength in numbers. Fourth, creator groups were looking to another institution, the telecomm regulator, for help even though the latter was not a front-line copyright institution. Fifth, the creator group was using the model of another country's copyright regime (France) in ways that would not have been central as recently as the mid-1980s.

Many of the features of this micro case are evident in the larger debate about how copyright is being affected by the emergence of the information highway, or somewhat more narrowly, the Internet. Several governmental and other institutional players have mounted major studies and task forces and conference proceedings. We look briefly at four of these (USA, EU, WIPO and Canada) in order to draw out the issues of change, the kinds of institutional change that are implied and partially underway, and the nature of the interests involved. There is clearly considerable overlap among the studies but also some national and international differences.

The information highway is not an exact concept but turns on several developments and the emergence of important new products and services linked to digitalisation. Within the world of telecommunications policy a key conundrum is the concept of 'convergence' (US Information Infrastructure Task Force, 1995). Broadcasting and telecommunications (telephone) worlds are converging into each other's market realms because of the colossal impact of digital technology and the array of new products and services it brings. But convergence also occurs between competition and intellectual property regulatory bodies and telecommunications regulators, especially since the vital politics of transition is centred on whether the competition allowed should be fulsome, fierce and free, or fair, workable and, in effect, 'managed' (Doern and Wilks, 1996). Thus convergence is fundamentally both a technological and an economic and political process which plays out differently in different countries (Crandall and Waverman, 1995; Thurow, 1997).

It is the uncertainty of the information highway's boundaries and numerous services and points of access that ultimately condition the copyright debate. Digitalisation makes available both faster and higher volumes of information transmittal and these are central to the formation and stunning growth of the information highway, whether they be in satellite, wireless, wire, cable or broadcast systems of communication. They also redefine how and where publishing occurs and where author and creator works can be marketed or their rights abused (Barlow, 1994; Burk, 1994; Symposium, 1994).

An important initial report is that of the US Working Group on Intellectual Property Rights of the Information Infrastructure Task Force (US Information Infrastructure Task Force, 1995). The task force process involved more than 150 organisations and individuals and included a special Conference on Fair Use involving 60 groups of users and creators. A Copyright Awareness Campaign was also launched. It is also of considerable importance to stress that US President Clinton was already giving special emphasis to the telecommunications and information industries as the dynamic engine of the US economy, an interest that culminated in his announced position in 1997 that the Internet should be declared from the outset to be a free trade zone of global commerce (*The Economist*, July 5, 1997, p. 15). The Task Force was looking at all intellectual property but there is little doubt that copyright was its main concern.

As it sought to preserve the balance between users and creators, the task force report first addressed and answered three questions about the nature of copyright and the information highway. First, it asked whether, as some assert, copyright protection should be reduced in the new milieu. This was posed because of public expectations that information would be and should be free. Its answer was that yes indeed, 'information per se should not be protected by copyright law ... nor is it', but that 'protection of works of authorship provides the stimulus for creativity' (US Information Infrastructure Task Force, 1995, p. 14).

A second question asked was whether technological advances justified reduced protection. Since unauthorised reproduction, adaptation, distribution and other uses were now extremely easy, the argument was that the law 'should legitimize those uses or face widespread flouting' (US Information Infrastructure Task Force, 1995, p. 15). The Task Force answer to this proposition was that it was invalid and that such acts, merely because they were possible, should not be condoned.

Finally, there was the third but related question that the information highway functioned in 'cyberspace' which was a sovereignty unto itself, and would/should be governed by its participants own ethics or 'netiquette'. This was a more extreme claim but, as we saw in the discussion in Chapter 6 of trademarks and Internet domain names, it is not entirely fanciful that Internet users see themselves functioning in a new form of democratic participative realm (Barlow, 1994; Elkins, 1995). The Task Force rejected the 'copyright Dodge City' model implied here but did recognise that there are many business models already in operation in the information highway. It noted that 'some content providers will choose not to enforce all – or any – of their rights; and others may change their business practices' (US Information Infrastructure Task Force, 1995, p. 15). But the task force concluded that effective copyright protection is a fundamental need.

There was also an implicit fourth question in the broad copyright–information highway agenda. Hence the US Task Force felt obliged to say that a new framework for copyright on the information highway did not require 'a dramatic increase in author's rights, such as more limited or no further applicability of the fair use doctrine' (US Information Infrastructure Task Force, 1995, p. 17). This was because some creator interests argued that as it was now technically feasible to meter each use of a copyrighted work, each use could and should be charged for. Hence, according to this view, fair use (free use?) should be a thing of the past.

As it addressed each of these questions the final position of the US Task Force was that existing copyright law in the USA needed only 'fine tuning' in the face of the new technologies but that triple attention had to be paid to:

- the law;
- the technology;
- education and awareness activities.

However, the pressure to obtain greater copyright protection in the USA has been significant, even without considerations of the Internet. In 1998 the US Congress was considering legislation that would extend by 20 years the term of copyright protection. Support for the bill is coming mainly from the film industry, music publishers and heirs. The justification is held to be that more protection will improve the US balance of trade, and compensate for lengthening life spans. As an editorial in the *New York Times* observed in opposition to this extension, 'the tendency is to vest the notion of creativity in the owners of copyright. But artists, including those who work for places like Disney, always emerge from the undifferentiated public' (*New York*

Times, February 23, 1998, p. 9). The editorial went on to defend the importance of the public domain by showing that this means 'nearly every work of any kind produced before the early 1920s are an essential part of every artist's sustenance, of every person's sustenance' (*New York Times*, February 23, 1998, p. 9).

A European perspective on copyright and the Internet can be gleaned initially from the previously mentioned Green Paper, which interestingly was cast as copyright in the 'Information Society'. We have already mentioned that European views of copyright are partially different in that civil law traditions give greater weight to the moral rights of creators and policy makers link copyright more directly to cultural policy. Hence casting the Green Paper at the level of 'society' rather than an information highway or infrastructure is not a narrow difference. It is also important to stress in the case of European copyright policy that it is the EU and member states that jointly have jurisdiction. In patents, the situation is, as we have seen, more institutionally complex in that the European Patent Office is not an EU institution. Trademarks are in the EU domain as mentioned in Chapter 6. This means that in copyright a wider set of EU players is involved than is typically the case in patents and trademarks.

The European Green Paper identifies many of the same causal forces that are changing the copyright milieu but it brought out features or expressed institutional needs with a different sense of priority and emphasis. For example, it noted that the law in force at present 'depends on a relatively strict separation between the different categories of work – musical works, literary works ... [and that] the forms of exploitation contemplated in the law as it stands are all based on a fairly slow rate of dissemination' (Commission of the European Communities, 1995, p. 26). The digital revolution was changing both these situations and hence the study gives the impression of the need for more than fine tuning. In part this may be due to the fact that civil law systems defined copyright more narrowly whereas Anglo-American legal traditions defined it more comprehensively in statute law. Far more than the US study, the European study also spoke of the much larger set of players that would function in the information society and hence would begin to affect copyright policy. This included a greater importance for the collective associations.

But European copyright policy and institutions would also be affected by three features which are almost by definition less endemic to the USA. First, Europe (or, more specifically, the EU) exhibits divided jurisdiction on copyright matters (and in other related areas such as telecommunications law). The EU has issued several directives on copyright but it does not have the field to itself since it is an entity composed of member nation states. Second, the digital revolution suggests overall the need for harmonisation of copyright laws within the EU but the EU must also obey the dictates of the principle of subsidiarity. This principle emphasises the need for decentralised solutions and for the Commission and EU to act only where the member nation states cannot act effectively. Third, there is a concern to maintain and enhance the internal market within the EU. The Green Paper expresses overtly a fear that copyright and related controls may endanger the internal market because of a 'relapse into fragmentation' (Commission of the European Communities, 1995, pp. 32–33). In other words, the information highway and the new telecommunications revolution would be seen as so crucial to each country individually that they would begin to regulate in response to the political pressures of both the winners and losers of Internet–copyright politics and thus undo some of the progress made in forging the internal market, the central achievement of the EU in the last decade (Anderson and Eliassen, 1993; McCormick, 1996; Greenwood and Aspinwall, 1998).

These concerns were borne out again early in 1998, when the European Commission set out plans by the European Union for an international communications 'charter' that was a response to the previously mentioned Clinton declaration of a free trade, deregulated global information highway (*Financial Times*, February 5, 1998, p. 20). The EU saw the need for cooperation on legal and technical issues that included copyright, data protection, taxation and control of pornography. The plans stress that 'it is not a new international organisation we are talking about but a flexible coordination mechanism [because] we need to be fleet of foot ourselves to match the nature of the industry' (quoted in *Financial Times*, February 5, 1998, p. 20).

From the USA and the EU we now turn briefly to a WIPO symposium report (WIPO, 1994). Of interest is the fact that the symposium involving 550 IP persons/ interests worldwide was cosponsored by WIPO and the French Ministry of Culture and Francophonie. Both the head of WIPO, Arpad Bogsch, and the French Minister of Culture, Jacques Toubon, made early reference in their statements to Le Chapelier who wrote in 1791 that intellectual property 'is the most sacred, the most legitimate and the most personal property' (WIPO, 1994, p. 19 and p. 23). This, combined with the fact that the symposium was being held in the Grand Louvre in Paris, was clearly intended to evoke the cultural roots of copyright and the moral rights of authors. The French Minister went on to state that this 'personalized concept of the creator's rights has always been a basis for our philosophy, for our principles on literary and artistic property ... and it has also helped anchor this part of private law firmly in the cultural domain' (Toubon, 1994, p. 24).

In line with the symposium's main focus, Toubon stressed that 'the enormous intermediate area between the initial author and the user having been disrupted by the new technologies, copyright must take this disruption into account' (Toubon, 1994, p. 25). He then went on to stress the possible 'risks of regression' which can accompany technical progress. One of these was the 'marginalization of independent creation' and another was the weakening of the position of creators 'compared with the holders of the new distribution and communication vectors' (Toubon, 1994, p. 26). There is little doubt that these views were expressed to counter the US commercial model of rights. Toubon also pointedly concluded by saying that 'although certain intellectual property rights do concern trade, the fruit of the creation of authors and the performances of actor and musicians cannot be assimilated to these acts of production and commerce' (Toubon, 1994, p. 27). He also stressed that the European Union had been able to safeguard this balance and emphasised that 'WIPO's vocation is to stand at the legal, industrial, and cultural crossroads, in collaboration with Unesco and the ILO, that are also the guardians of international agreements in closely related fields' (Toubon, 1994, p. 27).

If a European view of copyright and technology struck the initial themes of the symposium, there were also other views expressed. Some came in the form of overall contrasts between common law and civil law traditions and institutions but other responses about the core ideas behind copyright institutions were more direct and even visceral. Thus, in summary comments, Paul Goldstein, the noted US IP lawyer and scholar noted how 'some of the symposium's speakers have romanticized the artist starving in his garret, invoking the romantic images of *La Bohéme*' (Goldstein, 1994, p. 261). Goldstein said that to the extent that he relied on theory, he would take welfare economics as his text. He then observed that 'whatever its imperfections, economic theory does a far better job than any other in explaining the behaviour of those who produce and consume literary and artistic works' (Goldstein, 1994, p. 261). Thus in his view, artists do not starve in their garret because they want to, rather, 'every serious creator wants to communicate his work to as large an audience as his vision can command' and therefore 'copyright and author's right create the shelter of privacy that authors need, and give publishers and other risk-taking intermediaries the economic protection they need, to make this hoped-for communication between author and audience a reality' (Goldstein, 1994, p. 261).

This focus on core ideas about copyright institutions and their cultural versus economic traditions is not intended to suggest that the WIPO symposium did not discuss other very practical areas. Other areas such as the role of technology in solving technological problems about copyright and the implications for collective associations were also examined (Gyertyanfy, 1994; Parrot, 1994; Tournier, 1994). But the differences in ideas backed by political power are at the core of institutional change in copyright institutions internationally.

A final example of the range of discussion on copyright can be seen in a 1995 Canadian symposium (Department of Justice, Industry Canada, Canadian Heritage, 1995). It had a more narrowly based discussion than the US, EU and WIPO reports just noted, but, in one respect, it was also different because it contained more sceptical views about the adaptability of copyright laws and institutions to the onslaught of digital technology. For example, Pamela Samuelson, the American law professor, spoke more directly about the threat posed to copyright institutions. She referred not to the confident 'copyright is adaptable' argument advanced by the established copyright institutions in government and the legal profession but rather to those of 'well known and technically proficient persons who predict that the impact that digital technologies will have on copyright law is to cause its death' (Samuelson, 1995, p. 94). Such observers point to the 'status quo plus' thinking on copyright as being wedded to 'industrial age' thinking rather than 'information age' thinking. As Samuelson goes on to say, 'if copyright ultimately does not survive digital networked environments, it may be because control over copying in these environments may not be attainable . . . [that is, because] multiple copies can easily and cheaply be made and distributed throughout the world' (Samuelson, 1995, p. 95).

As at all moments of major change, those advocating a new institutional regime do not have a well-developed alternative paradigm and hence established institutions have the upper hand. But it is clear that, compared to its earlier eras or phases of technological adaptation, copyright institutions are being forced by digital technology to a much greater extent to question their basic concepts and underlying capacities.

Conclusions

This chapter has examined copyright regulatory institutions in a three-step manner:

- in relation to long-established international treaties such as the Berne Convention;
- as a distinct regime that is more pluralistic than the patent and trademark regime;
- through recent discussion and debate about the institutional impact of digitalisation and the Internet and information highway on copyright institutions and ideas.

Unlike the patent or trademark process the creator of copyrighted works does not in most countries have formally to register to have his or her creations approved. A copyright exists from the moment a work is created and is, moreover, endowed with a tradition of both moral and economic rights. National copyright systems follow the broad contours of world copyright regimes in this regard and also involve a structure of institutions and interests that is by definition more pluralistic and dispersed, particularly because of the involvement of cultural ministries and interests.

The analysis reiterates that there are basic differences of view at the global level that arise between countries governed by traditions of civil law where copyright is embedded in a cultural view and those with common law or Anglo-American traditions where it is seen more as an economic right. These differences are, if anything, heightened by the need to confront the new realities of digitalisation, the information highway and globalisation. The chapter's focus on a US versus French polarisation of views should not be taken to mean that it is only those countries which hold these views. A larger European view is being debated within the EU where the institutional picture is also different compared to patents because patents are centred on a non-EU agency. WIPO also represents a further distribution of these views where, among developing countries, concerns range from the protection of folklore to the globalisation of culture through the Internet.

The discussion of the newer dual interplay between copyright and trade, and copyright and digital technology has been given a necessary initial look in the earlier analysis, but it is by no means complete. We need now to examine the WTO and TRIPs and how it drives the institutional politics of IP in general and copyright in particular, both internationally and within national governments.

CHAPTER EIGHT

The Emerging Role of the WTO: Trade-related IP and Relations with WIPO

The final area of institutional change impacting on the core functions of IP agencies is the establishment of the World Trade Organization (WTO) and its Trade-Related Intellectual Property (TRIPs) Agreement signed as part of the Uruguay Round Final Act. TRIPs is the main aspect of the WTO in which this chapter is interested. Accordingly, its main direct impacts in terms of this book are on the World Intellectual Property Organization (WIPO). But it also affects the national IP offices institutionally in that the WTO developments have national counterpart effects felt in the form of the greater overall influence of trade departments within national governments and then on IP agencies. 'Trade-related' is the operative term here in that there is, relative to a decade ago, a kind of trade community hegemony that is driving the IP agendas in each country. In short, traditional IP policy makers are now reacting to the trade policy community rather than the reverse.

However, also underlying the global politics of the WTO–TRIPs arrangements are the basic IP policy trade-offs that reside among countries, especially as between developing and developed countries. As we have seen, when core IP policy trade-offs between IP protection and IP dissemination are visualised among nations it is clear that country-to-country differences in preferred policies could be justified depending upon whether a country's policy makers saw it as a country that was directly an 'innovating' one or was a country engaged largely in 'imitation' (Trebilcock and Howse, 1995, p. 251).

Thus, even with the TRIPs accord in place, these differences are not resolved. Many economists are perhaps only now joining the debate but many agree that full harmonisation does not make sense. Frischtak concludes for example that 'there is little in economic theory to support convergence of IPR systems on a cross-country basis, particularly if convergence means an increase in the level of protection in developing and industrializing countries' (Frischtak, 1995, p. 201). Even the quasi-populist American economist, Lester Thurow, argues that for IP 'one size doesn't fit all' (Thurow, 1997, p. 102). He sees the need for a global system of IP rights but points out for example that 'the Third World's need to get low-cost pharmaceuticals is not equivalent to its need for low-cost CDs' (Thurow, 1997, p. 103).

Because the WTO–TRIPs developments are recent, this chapter of necessity can offer only an initial and tentative account of institutional change. First, we describe the essence of the WTO and TRIPs agreement and convey further some of the underlying politics of their creation. Second, we look at early developments centred on the activities of the TRIPs Council. Third, we examine the overall relations between the WTO and WIPO. Finally, we examine the national manifestations mentioned earlier of trade community influences on traditional national IP institutions.

The WTO and TRIPs: key features and political origins

Since 1947 the General Agreement on Tariffs and Trade (GATT) has never had what its original designers then had planned for, a full-fledged organisation to oversee it. GATT was officially a temporary arrangement. Several GATT 'rounds' of negotiations had fashioned an ever more complex agreement agreed to by an ever larger number of countries. A bureaucracy, the GATT Secretariat, had been built in Geneva and dispute-settlement processes had gradually evolved but not the long-planned governing organisation. The Uruguay Round finally completed the long-delayed plan. The WTO was established to 'oversee an integrated dispute settlement regime and to undertake a pro-active trade policy surveillance role' (Trebilcock and Howse, 1995, p. 38).

The WTO is composed of all the member GATT countries and it is different from the previous GATT bureaucracy in three respects (Hoekman and Kostecki, 1995). First, it is more integrative in that the Uruguay Round agreement is itself broader, encompassing trade in areas not covered at all in GATT deals or not covered as extensively. These areas include TRIPs as well as areas such as services, investment, and agriculture. Indeed, the WTO would coordinate three related institutional components: the Goods Council; the Services Council; and the TRIPs Council (see later).

Second, it is more integrated in that the dispute-settlement mechanisms were intended to cover these wider realms as well as concerns regarding traditional trade in goods and tariffs, and the dispute-settlement system was to have more teeth and to work more expeditiously. Dispute resolutions would have a strict time limit established for the conclusion of the process and a single member would be prevented from blocking the adoption of reports of trade-dispute panels, or, on appeal, of appellate bodies.

Third, its pro-activeness would be manifest in the WTO's ability to itself have a trade policy review mechanism in which it would have an independent investigative authority to initiate rotating country-by-country reviews of international and domestic policies that might adversely impact on trade relationships among countries. If this pro-active role were successful, the need for dispute settlement might decline over time. All of these provisions centred on the WTO would, it was hoped, lessen the tendency of some governments, especially the USA, to use unilateral trade actions to harass trade from other competing countries.

During the Uruguay Round, the issue of mandates in IP between the WIPO and the proposed World Trade Organization generated considerable dispute (Trebilcock and Howse, 1995). The developing countries preferred the WIPO as the lead institution because it had facilitated diverse IP policies and institutions in developing countries. The USA and Europe, but especially the former, wanted a stronger WTO mandate because it wanted better dispute settlement and enforcement of IP rights, particularly regarding key developing countries whose regimes were weak either in law or in the implementation of those laws. As a result, the Uruguay Final Round

Act includes for the first time not only the WTO itself but also a comprehensive agreement on TRIPs that, in principle, seeks to balance the conflicting values inherent in IP and between developed and developing countries.

For our purposes six key provisions of the Uruguay Round TRIPs provisions are important:

1   a statement of general principles and of the interaction of the agreement with the Paris and Berne Conventions;
2   substantive norms regarding the protection of the basic kinds of intellectual property;
3   obligations concerning domestic enforcement of IP rights;
4   obligations regarding the facilitation in domestic legal systems of the acquisition and maintenance of IP rights;
5   dispute settlement;
6   a WTO-based framework for TRIPs (Hoekman and Kostecki, 1995; Trebilcock and Howse, 1995; Drahos, 1996).

The TRIPs Agreement brings intellectual property rights more fully into the ambit of such core trade principles as national treatment and most favoured nation obligations. There are some exceptions to these as set out in the existing IP treaties such as the Paris, Berne and Rome Conventions. Article 7's statement of objectives captures the balance inherent in the IP trade-off among countries by stating that 'the protection and enforcement of intellectual property rights should contribute to the promotion and technological innovation and to the transfer and dissemination of technology'. It goes on to say that this should be 'to the mutual advantage of producers and users of technological knowledge and in a manner conducive to social and economic welfare' (TRIPs Agreement, Article 7).

The TRIPs Agreement sets out standards concerning the availability, scope and use of IP rights for each of:

- copyright and related rights;
- trademarks;
- geographical indications;
- industrial designs;
- patents;
- lay-out designs (topographies) of integrated circuits;
- protection of undisclosed information;
- control of anticompetitive practices in contractual licences.

The agreement then also specifies the crucial enforcement obligations and issues regarding IP. These include civil and administrative procedures and remedies, border measures and criminal procedures.

The TRIPs Agreement refers to both 'dispute prevention and settlement'. It calls for transparent processes regarding laws, regulations and final judicial and administrative rulings, and an obligation of member states to notify the TRIPs Council regarding national laws that deal with or affect IP matters. General GATT–WTO dispute-settlement procedures apply to IP, with the crucial exception that developing countries have a period of 5 years (until 2000) before these procedures apply to them.

As with any complex international agreement, there are many detailed provisions that are also a part of the TRIPs Agreement. But TRIPs unmistakably puts the 'trade' in IP and brings the WTO into IP policy and decision making in ways that did not exist before.

The TRIPs Council: early developments

Institutionally, the TRIPs Agreement creates a new entity, the Council on Trade Related Aspects of Intellectual Property Rights (TRIPs Council). The Council is charged with the monitoring of domestic compliance with the agreement but it is not directly involved in dispute settlement. The general provisions of GATT will apply to disputes under TRIPs and thus, as we have seen, they are more closely linked with the strengthened dispute-settlement role of the World Trade Organization.

An understanding of the TRIPs institutions including the Council for TRIPs must be rooted in a somewhat deeper understanding of the way in which it emerged on the Uruguay GATT Round negotiating agenda. As we have seen, the issue was very much a US one in that the USA had put it on the agenda in 1984. GATT had previously dealt with some IP issues, but since about 1978 these had been confined to trade in counterfeit goods and hence were quite narrowly constrained. Both in 1984, and certainly by 1986, the US had quite a broad understanding about what it meant by 'trade-related' IP. It encompassed both strong standards and viable enforcement regimes. However, other developed countries were more uncertain about what should be included, in part because of turf wars within national governments and among countries (e.g. within the EU). By 1988, however, the European Union was firmly on side. The delay in reaching an EU consensus was in part tied to larger trade policy and political stances. France, for example, was particularly concerned about the overall US trade agenda, in part because France feared that EU agricultural subsidies would be a special target. The EU and other countries were, by the same token, also concerned about the need to keep the US content within the GATT rather than send the USA off on still more bouts of aggressive unilateralism in their trade policy.

Critics of the TRIPs agreement are in no doubt about how it came into being. Legal scholars such as Peter Drahos argue that TRIPs represents 'hard law' in every sense but that 'it was not the product of carefully coordinated economic analysis' (Drahos, 1997, p. 201). Instead, 'it was the manifestation of rent-seeking desires of those multinationals that saw opportunities for themselves in redefining and globalizing intellectual property rights' (Drahos, 1997, p. 201). Political economist Susan K. Sell also sees these developments regarding intellectual property as a direct result of a 'coercive US strategy to force recalcitrant countries to pass laws strengthening intellectual property protection' (Sell, 1995, p. 316).

As mentioned, the other key feature of US-led pressure was to make intellectual property 'GATTable' by which was meant bring it under dispute settlement in the new WTO. Thus in institutional terms IP dispute settlement was brought in through the new WTO panel processes while other key issues were structured through the newly created Council for TRIPs (Getlan, 1995).

The Council is composed of all members of the WTO supported by a very small secretariat of only four professional staff. WIPO is invited to all meetings, as are other major international bodies (WTO, 1996). In its early stages of operation, the Council for TRIPs has evolved two basic approaches. The first approach is systemic and centres on the many TRIPs requirements for member countries' notification of laws and policies. The second approach involves a three-step process for dealing with specific issues that may be raised by WTO members.

With regard to the systemic notification of laws, many Council meetings have been taken up in discussing the extent to which notification is occurring. This is implementation activity that is done on a country-by-country and subject-by-subject basis. Assessments are done mainly by fellow member countries rather than by the staff of the WTO/Council on TRIPs. Not surprisingly, it is the larger countries such as the USA, EU and Japan that have the resources to check into the other countries' practices and notification activity. This very detailed activity has been laborious but very necessary. It has helped some countries to obtain feedback on legislation which they may be in the process of drafting and it serves in some general way as an educational process for everyone involved.

The 1996 report of the Council for TRIPs summarises the six meetings held in 1996 and shows the not unexpected array of start-up issues and progress inherent in the TRIPs political bargain (WTO, 1996). Some 30 member countries had notified all or some of their implementing legislation. Members were being asked to provide responses to a checklist of issues on enforcement. Developing country members were pointing out their difficulty in notifying in many areas because of constraints on their resources. A workshop on border enforcement was also being organised.

With respect to the Council's second basic process, the handling of special issues, the three steps involved are both old and new, old in the sense that familiar GATT processes are involved, and new in the sense that the Council may be involved at mid-stage in these processes. Thus, first, member countries that raise a specific IP issue are expected to deal with it on a bilateral or country-to-country basis. Most issues are solved in this manner. A second recourse is a mid-stage one, through referring a matter to the Council on TRIPs. Finally, resort to WTO panels and dispute-settlement processes is possible. Three IP cases have been resolved before the panel stage and one has gone to a panel. In the case of dispute settlement and panels as such, the Council for TRIPs has no role or jurisdiction.

With regard to the generic issues with which the WTO and the Council for TRIPs have had to deal, some could be seen as being a built-in agenda from the entire TRIPs negotiation. Preeminent in this area of the agenda is the enforcement issue. Geographical indicators were also built in at the insistence of the wine countries and industries, and issues such as trade secrets have emerged more strongly than expected.

As already mentioned, developing countries have a five-year lead time into any TRIPs dispute-settlement requirements and thus the focus in the interim in particular has been on ensuring that enforcement regimes are built or strengthened. This meant major commitments to training and education in customs administration, courts, judges and related regulatory institutions. In some cases, new laws were needed but training was also seen as being geared to developing continuous sensitivity to IP issues at the sharp end of compliance and enforcement.

Enforcement of intellectual property rights in general is obviously crucial since if the rights are not credible and infringements occur there is no incentive to acquire them and hence to innovate (World Intellectual Property Organization, 1994a; 1995). The rights holder must be able to take action against infringers and there must be recourse to state authorities to deal with counterfeits. The courts are accordingly a crucial feature, largely operating under civil law but criminal law is also important. Equally, however, it is important to view IP enforcement as going well beyond litigation or the threat of litigation. The broader compliance underpinnings involve:

- the right holder's own knowledge of its competitor's practices;
- the opposition process provided for in the application or registration process;
- the use of negotiation, mediation and alternative dispute-settlement mechanisms.

The value of these broader compliance approaches lies especially in the knowledge that the cost of actual litigation can be extremely expensive with very uncertain outcomes.

Enforcement and compliance have always been important in IP areas as a whole but it is primarily in the international enforcement of copyrights in which the key IP institutions have seen the most change. As pointed out in Chapter 7 there are some obligations of states to provide for adequate enforcement of international copyright and neighbouring rights in the Berne, Rome and Phonograms Conventions administered through WIPO but these were not extensive. WIPO was aware of these inadequacies and throughout the 1980s had many meetings on these issues, particularly regarding piracy (World Intellectual Property Organization, 1994). But, as we have seen, WIPO proceeded very cautiously, in part because of its internal political need to balance the interests of developing countries and developed countries.

It was the USA that became most exasperated by the slowness of progress and by the continuing piracy that it saw going on in key developing countries. The USA employed many elements of its agressive unilateralist trade policy to bring copyright (and other IP measures) into the realm of trade policy and trade negotiation. Chief among these was the use of the so-called Special 301 provision of the Omnibus Trade and Competitiveness Act of 1988. It provided for US trade sanctions against countries that the USA deemed were engaged in unfair trade practices. Under the 301 weapon, the USA began listing the IP sins of several developing countries, as well as other selected unfair practices of other trading partners (Bhagwati and Patrick, 1990; Getlan, 1995; Sell, 1995; Trebilcock and Howse, 1995).

The WTO–WIPO relationship

Thus it is in this realm of activity that one must reinsert the role of WIPO in the new WTO–WIPO institutional equation. WIPO was not at all enthusiastic about TRIPs and the impending WTO–Council role. At some points there was a fear in WIPO that it would be left out entirely. Given its far greater expertise, personnel and financial resources, this was an exaggerated fear but WIPO did lose political clout in the eyes of key players such as the USA and the EU.

Nonetheless, once the new regime was a fait accompli, WIPO and the WTO have settled into a basic relationship governed by an agreement between the two bodies. For WIPO, the coming of TRIPs, coincident with a change in its leadership in 1997, has forced on it what some of its senior officials have called a more integrated approach to intellectual property. This kind of thinking is evident in four areas of activity.

The first is simply the new de facto importance of the enforcement and implementation role in the overall international IP realm. The emphasis has to be on the system bringing those who break the IP rules to the courts of member countries both speedily and effectively. The second is that the training role that WIPO has always carried out has to give relatively more emphasis to training the trainers and to fostering greater inter-regional exchange. This implies a greater investment which ultimately must come from WIPO revenues or from special infusions of funding and personnel from the developed countries.

A third area of broadening is that WIPO is likely to have to deal more with the sweep of IP economics. Some member countries claim that what they need more of from WIPO is in the realm of supplying full economic rationales and argument as to why better IP regimes need to be established and complied with. The greatest difficulty is often in persuading ministers within their own countries. In the last two decades WIPO's advisory role has been, in the view of many, too narrowly legislative in focus, and even with this ambit, has always dealt with whether laws were compatible with the treaties that WIPO administered. This focus has been described by one observer interviewed by the author as being 'severely neutral'. Some of the pressure to broaden the economic base of advice came directly from developing countries in South and East Asia rather than developed country members.

Last, but hardly least, WIPO is aware that it must broaden the way it views the computerisation of IP information and its links to the Internet. Extensive computerisation has occurred in the last 15 years but the more integrated needs come in several different ways. In the realm of training it means not only technical training in a hardware and software sense but also changing the culture of operation in the wider sense in which whole IP organisations need to be transformed. This is an issue both for WIPO's own operations and for member countries and their patent and trademark offices.

In some ultimate sense, the Internet can mean that access to IP information is universal, can be downloaded anywhere, and thus suggests directionally at least, that there is less need for national offices and systems and more need for regional and world IP entities. Hence the issue of competing and cooperating IP agencies is again joined.

All of these issues found their way into the initial speeches of the new Director General of WIPO, Dr Kamil Idris in the fall of 1997 (WIPO, 1997d, 1997e). To a much greater extent than his predecessor would have done, Idris indicated the need for change cast both in the nature of technological change and the economics of IP but also in the context of WIPO as a unique organisation. He described WIPO as unique in 'having a dual character as both an intergovernmental organization which serves the interests and needs of a community of states, and a global market-oriented organization which serves the needs of a large, dynamic and growing market of users' (WIPO, 1997d, p. 1).

Not all of the changes mentioned are caused simply by the formation of the WTO and TRIPs. Internet issues are clearly technologically centred but are occurring simultaneously with the WTO–TRIPs relationship. And the changes are also coinciding, as indicated by the Idris speeches, with a change in the leadership of WIPO. Arpad Bogsch's long tenure has ended and in its wake is emerging Idris' broader sense of review and self-criticism by WIPO's staff itself. The changes of focus are a part of this transformation but they also only partially reflect the size of the task in building up a fully fledged IP regime, especially a compliance regime for IP relations between the developed and developing countries. This is still a massive undertaking in which the essential international agency reality is that the WTO has the political power and WIPO has the technical and financial resources.

While there are generic across-the-board compliance issues that cover all areas – patents, copyright and trademarks – there are also difficult areas of particular importance within these realms. Thus, in trademarks there are special problems with the previously mentioned geographic designations. In copyright, there are wide-ranging issues for enforcing the rights of smaller performers. Hollywood and other big performance interests can take care of themselves but small performers have much greater difficulty. Above all, in copyright there are special problems with enforcing antipiracy provisions. The Americans in particular have maintained massive pressure on countries such as China for its failure to go after offending plants and firms. Recently, however, such pressure has paid off and the USA praised China 'for shutting down 39 factories and production facilities producing CDs and CD-Roms' and making 'more than 250 arrests' (*Financial Times*, May 1, 1997, p. 4).

Undoubtedly less headline making in nature, but equally crucial over the long term, are the problems that developing countries face in building underlying copyright institutions, often from the ground up. Some of this was already underway within the WIPO ambit in the last decade. For example, in 1986 there were 76 countries that were signatories to the Berne Convention. By 1997, there were 125. As a result, WIPO has had numerous regional and subregional workshops, training and other events throughout Africa and South America. The nature of copyright institutions established or being built have varied widely and must inevitably take into account varied national histories and traditions. This is especially the case for developing collective society administrations among diverse cultural and performer groups. Much of this institution building has also had to occur amid the need to adjust to the fast developing Internet technologies, creating for many developing countries a kind of double 'catch-up problem' with all its resource and personnel constraints.

Some of these changes may also make WIPO the institutional arena through which challenges to the US-dominated WTO arena are mounted politically and analytically. Drahos argues that the processes of thinking more strategically about IP laws and systems may only now be beginning in the face of US hegemony. Even within TRIPs he identifies seven strategies that might be considered:

- non-compliance;
- loopholes;
- soft law;
- counterproposal;
- economic transparency;

- the independent umpire;
- hard law (Drahos, 1997, pp. 204–210).

There are clearly different 'pros and cons' to these for different countries and combinations of countries but strategic responses are bound to occur.

An economic transparency strategy, for example, might force more economic analysis to be carried out and made public regarding the transaction and other costs of protection under TRIPs. Drahos, for example, argues that the Council for TRIPs should establish a cost review mechanism the purpose of which would be to 'track the costs to states of implementing TRIPs, the effects on consumers in terms of increased prices [and] the anticompetitive effects of TRIPs' (Drahos, 1997, p. 208).

Another example, this time of a hard law counterstrategy from key developing countries, could be one where they pick their own ground to emulate what the USA did for its computer chip industry. Key developing countries such as India, China and Indonesia might legislate for a *sui generis* form of protection for indigenous knowledge within its borders, with such knowledge defined broadly to include the physical, cultural and social resources of its indigenous peoples. This would then be negotiated with developed countries.

Clearly, all such strategies and conceptions of action through WIPO, the WTO and the Council on TRIPs, depend on many factors and bases of political power and agency agendas but the global issues of IP generated by TRIPs are undoubtedly subject to considerable change, now that IP is one of the key international economic policy weapons of choice.

Broader trade community influence within nation states

While our attention in this chapter is on the WTO, TRIPs, the TRIPs Council and their relations with WIPO, there is a need to show the other manifestations of a trade influence that are occurring within member nation states of both the WTO and WIPO, including our four-country sample. Trade policy communities are exerting greater influence over their IP counterparts in most major developed countries. And this influence centres overwhelmingly on the protection aspects of IP. The precise conduit for these influences varies in each country depending upon how its ministries and trade and industrial and IP policy functions are structured but the key overall causal arrows are unmistakeably clear.

The political dynamic starts with key US IP industry interests who see IP-centred industries as an US comparative advantage and who apply pressure on that government to protect and assert those interests (Merges, 1990; Sell, 1995). Within the US Government, the Office of the US Trade Representative has become the focal point of such pressure and it in turn leads the US pressure on the rest of the world with the evident tactics of first, aggressive unilateralism, and now through the WTO–TRIPs, American-led aggressive multilateralism.

The tentacles have extended and evolved in other jurisdictions. The European Union caught on quickly with its trade community having not only the example of US practices but also the advantage that trade matters were one of the few areas within EU law where the EU could speak for and negotiate on behalf of all its member states.

Other individual developed countries such as Australia and Canada experienced similar intra-governmental shifts of power in agenda setting. For example, in Canada, in the 1990s in particular, the Department of Foreign Affairs and International Trade (DFAIT) and Industry Canada both became trade-oriented agenda setters. Both are 'trade' departments in that the former has basic legal and foreign policy jurisdiction while the latter has sectoral industry expertise as well as responsibilities for investment and trade promotion. To this core duo one could easily add the Department of Finance and thus a powerful trio of voices existed whose stances when applied to IP are far more on the protection side of the IP trade-off. A key related reason for this political-institutional reality in North America is that since 1986 there has been virtually continuous trade negotiations starting with the FTA, then NAFTA and finally the GATT–WTO. This means that the core dynamic of decision making has been that of a relatively centralised negotiation rather than policy making carried out sectorally in more self-contained departments and policy communities.

Conclusions

This chapter has traced the emergence of the WTO and the TRIPs Agreement as a crucial new 1990s element of IP institutional relations. We have also looked at the early start-up work of the TRIPs Council as it seeks above all to ensure that member countries comply with both the establishment and effective implementation of IP laws and regimes. Clearly, these new institutions have altered the configurations of both power and partnership among international and national IP bodies, especially between the WTO and WIPO.

The analysis has shown that the essential reality is that the WTO has the political muscle centred in its dispute-settlement provisions which now apply to IP matters and that WIPO has the resources and expertise. The WTO's muscle is essentially backed by US tenacity and by a further residual use of US aggressive unilateralism. However, the TRIPs Council staff is small and WIPO is the organisation that must deliver the real resources in cooperation with many dozens of developing countries. These developing countries often have to construct IP institutions from the ground up and in a systemic way that embraces the full array of IP compliance arenas and sites, from the courts and police to border inspections and culturally centred collective associations needed to give meaning to copyright and other IP protection.

While these developments show the power of US trade strategy, it is more than likely that WIPO, the Council on TRIPs and other arenas will produce counter-strategies and debates that bring to the fore a more complete and transparent understanding of IP both in its protection and dissemination aspects for diverse developed and developing countries.

CHAPTER NINE

Conclusions

Global change is propelling most areas of public policy and most governing institutions. Intellectual property has clearly not escaped this overall set of pressures and indeed has been elevated to a new prominence by them. The many and complex interacting effects of global change have been the backdrop to this book and have found their way into different aspects of our account. The emergence of a knowledge economy has brought changing conceptions of science and technology policies and activities as well as trade, industrial and innovation policy. Digital technologies have changed both the economy and society. Governments and their agencies have sought to reinvent themselves both to cope with change and to influence it.

In the context of these larger forces, the central purpose of this book has been to provide an institutional examination of the nature of, and relationships among, four national and three international intellectual property agencies. The analytical focus has been on a middle-level institutional approach to examine change in the last decade in the operations of international and national IP regulators which are adapting to, and being buffeted by, the pressures of the globalised political economy and by reinvented government. The book has shown that while intellectual property policy is moving front and centre as a feature of national industrial and innovation policies, intellectual property institutions are much less well-known and analytically understood.

Given that IP literature and analysis has been dominated by technical, legal and economic disciplines, this book has sought to provide a complementary institutional focus derived from quite basic analysis in political science and public administration but augmented by the compelling need to examine both national and international IP governing and regulatory bodies and hence national-international institutional dynamics.

While the book has provided a more integrated middle-level look at IP institutions than any available at present, we have been careful to point out the limitations of the analysis as well. First, among the four realms of IP policy and operations, the focus has been primarily on patents, and secondarily on trademarks and copyright. Industrial designs have not been covered. Copyright institutions and issues have been examined but mainly in terms of how the combined trade-copyright-enforcement agenda has affected the broad political and institutional relations among IP institutions, including the World Trade Organization. Second, we have by no means examined all IP institutions as such in that this would include a macro-level approach to overall systems of law and other ministries and elements of the state including the courts and related enforcement processes. Ours has been a middle-level focus on IP agencies. Third, although we have referred to many policy issues inherent in the functioning of IP institutions, this book is not a book on IP policy as such. Issues such as the relations between IP and other policy fields including competition policy, environmental policy, telecommunications and health care policy have not, therefore, been fully examined.

The middle-level institutional focus has been devised more as a vehicle for applied analysis than as a concerted contribution to the broader theory of institutions. In looking at key features of national and international agencies, the central purpose has been to provide a basic look at IP institutions. Unlike other well-tilled policy fields, there was a need for this kind of basic institutional mapping in intellectual property policy.

The seven agencies examined have, of course, histories and lives of their own but we have been interested in them less as individual agencies than as a sample group of interacting agencies subject to similar changes. WIPO and the WTO have exhibited a particular institutional relationship largely because the former has been an agency with a more balanced mandate between developing and developed countries, while the latter, in respect of IP at least, has been a creature of developed country and especially US political power. The EPO shares features with the other two international bodies but has been shown to function in a more sheltered context. But it too is affected by WIPO and its business strategies. The four national bodies exhibit their own particular concerns in this evolving nexus of relationships. The UK Patent Office strategies vis-à-vis the EPO. The Canadian and Australian offices, as smaller IP offices in smaller countries, concern themselves more with future survival and possibly quite significant changes in roles. The USPTO evolves under the pressure of the aggressive US IP-trade-related strategy but, as an agency, even it has concerns about how it adjusts to a widening degree of political and clientele exposure and debate.

The conclusions to the analytical journey proceed in two stages, first with a brief recapitulation of the analysis and then with observations about the four key issues regarding IP institutional change and reform set out in Chapter 1.

Analytical summary

The organisation of the book has been based on the need to provide, in stages, the basic features of an overall IP institutional portrait. The IP institutional realm is, in reality, a more than a 100-year-old set of very complex macro treaty and legal arrangements with this book focusing mainly on the last decade of change. In Chapter 1 two aspects of middle-level institutional analysis were set out. The first referred to the core policy trade-offs inherent in any IP regulatory regime and how trade-off can legitimately vary among countries at different stages of economic development and, crucially, in relation to the varied power and influence of core IP interests including business, the IP professions and the state and its various ministries. The second aspect centred on some key features of the relations between national and international agencies and bureaucracies, about which more will be said later.

In Chapter 2 we focused in a descriptive manner on the basic cycle for dealing with patent applications. This cycle is at the core of the regulatory life of an IP agency and largely defines the technically dominated culture of the agency. Chapter 2 also set out the basic statutory and policy-derived mandates of the selected national and

international institutions. Chapter 3 then examined how the basic governing structures had evolved in the 1990s bringing out not only the expected crucial differences
between national and international bodies but also other aspects of institutional
change and stability, including:

- the recent shifts to reinvented executive or special operating agency status;
- changes in basic policy functions;
- the changing place of IP in national industrial and economic policies.

The policy changes were cast broadly as a steady movement away from traditional
industrial policy towards innovation policies but with the latter still of uncertain
shape and content.

Chapters 4 and 5 added a second layer of institutional analysis in that they took us
into a somewhat more detailed look at patents, first at the protection role, and then
at the dissemination role inherent in the overall IP trade-off. Five aspects and
processes in the protection role were explored:

- the quality and efficiency of pendency rates;
- issues and debates regarding the length of patent protection and IP protection in
  general;
- international enforcement and compliance issues;
- the role of big business in giving focus to the protection function;
- the role of the IP professions as intermediary interests between inventors and the
  IP agencies but whose primary interest is also in the protection function.

In Chapter 5 we examined the IP dissemination role in both its old and new
manifestations. In its newer guise the chapter showed how IP agencies are seeking to
play a dissemination role in three related senses in the 1990s:

- that of making existing IP information available to users;
- the possible dissemination of new value-added IP information;
- efforts to reach businesses and inventive sources which are not yet filing
  patents.

These dissemination roles were shown to cluster around a somewhat different set
of interests, including less readily organised small and medium-sized business
interest groups, and broader innovation institutions including universities.

A third layer of IP institutional analysis emerged in the next three chapters.
Chapter 6 showed that trademarks are the second line of business for most IP
agencies (especially the national agencies) ranking behind the core patent business
both in the volume of business and revenues they generate and in the inherent
prestige of the activity within the agency's organisational culture. The nature of the
trademark application and approval process also sets it apart from patents in that, at
its core, it is more of an art than a science and technology-centred process of
judgements and decisions. This feature is also central to why trademark examiners
within IP agencies and trademark agents in the larger IP profession have a greater
struggle for recognition and inherent status than their patent-based colleagues.

The trademark aspects of IP regimes are also characterised by a somewhat lesser
developed set of internationalised processes compared to patents. This is partly due
to the considerable importance of the language of commerce which seems to be

greater in trademark matters. But it is also due to the fact that trademarks can exist to some extent without being registered. Moreover, the trademark process is influenced by a wider array of industrial sectors and ranges of small and large firms than is the case with patents and thus makes it more of a national and even local matter for firms who might never patent but who could be involved in trademarks as a part of their more basic marketing and commercial activities.

The examination of copyright regulatory institutions was cast initially as only a tertiary part of the book in that the full cast of copyright institutions are simply not covered. This is because the national IP agencies examined tend to have only small copyright roles. But in other respects, the copyright issues have been crucial to the analysis.

Chapter 7 has shown how they are rooted in long-established international treaties such as the Berne Convention. It also showed that the copyright regime in most countries is more pluralistic than the patent regime and also the trademark regime. Chapter 7 also reviewed some broad institutional aspects of the discussion and debate about the impact of digitalisation and the information highway on the copyright regime. Furthermore, it was stressed that unlike the patent or trademark process the creator of copyrighted works does not have to register formally to have his or her creations approved. A copyright exists from the moment a work is created and, moreover, is endowed with both a tradition of moral and economic rights. National copyright systems were shown to follow the broad contours of world copyright regimes in this regard and to involve a structure of institutions and interests that is by definition more pluralistic and dispersed particularly because of the involvement of cultural ministries and interests and diverse collective associations needed to administer copyright policies and laws.

We also highlighted differences of view at the global level that arise between countries governed by traditions of civil law where copyright is embedded in a cultural view and those with common law or Anglo-American traditions where it is seen more as an economic right. These differences are, if anything, heightened by the need to confront the new realities of digitalisation, the information highway and globalisation. As indicated the chapter's focus on a USA versus France polarisation of these views should not be taken to mean that it is only those countries which hold these views. A larger European view is being debated within the EU where the institutional picture is also different compared to patents because patents are centred on a non-EU agency. WIPO also represents a further distribution of these views where, among developing countries, concerns range from the protection of folklore to fears about the globalisation of culture through the Internet.

Lastly, Chapter 8 traced the emergence of the WTO and the TRIPs Agreement as a crucial new 1990s element of IP institutional relations. It also examined the early start-up work of the TRIPs Council as it seeks above all to ensure that member countries comply with both the establishment and effective implementation of IP laws and regimes. Clearly, these new institutions have altered the configurations of both power and partnership among international and national IP bodies, especially between the WTO and WIPO.

Issues in the nature of IP institutional change

Although the main purpose of this book has been to bring a basic political-institutional and public administrative perspective to the much larger interdisciplinary realm of intellectual property literature, its basic approach may also be suggestive of the kinds of work needed when examining the growing inter-relations between national and international agencies. No claims of conceptual breakthroughs are made in this regard since IP issues was our overriding focus, and not the theory of institutions.

But the book does show that those who study domestic policy institutions and those who examine international institutions need to deal with each other's analytical worlds and problems to a much greater extent than has occurred to date. Chapter 1 stressed that international relations scholars were moving somewhat towards a more careful look at international entities as organisations, but that these steps were still tentative because of the larger overriding analytical concerns about power among nation states. Equally, scholars of domestic or national public policy have tended too often to treat international institutions and international agencies as only contextual elements in their analyses.

The nature of this book made analytical movement in both directions a compulsory task. But we have done so in a pragmatic way by examining some standard aspects of institutional and agency analysis:

- regulatory or production cycles and resultant agency cultures;
- the ranges of other service and advisory functions that are central to mandates;
- financing and issues related to the political saliency of the agency in its immediate ministry or other governing structures;
- system-wide pressures for the reinvention of government.

Such basic middle-level analysis is likely to be more and more necessary to make any basic sense of the growing globalisation of public policy and governing institutions. The concluding discussion that follows of the four issues demonstrates why this is necessary.

Inevitably in a book of this kind, the conclusions reached from and through the above layered structure of middle-level analysis range from those which are strong and well-supported by the evidence and others that are more in the category of observations that flow from the author's judgement about the nature of change and the balance of probabilities in the future. The concluding observations presented broadly emerge out of the four key elements of middle-level institutional analysis set out in Chapter 1 which focus on changing relations between national and international IP agencies:

1   the greater exposure of the tension inherent in the IP trade-off caused by the combined effects of globalisation, US hegemony in the IP agenda, and the pressure to reinvent government;

2   the continuing dominance of the protection role in the core technical cultures of the main IP agencies;

3   the financial interdependence of national and international IP offices and its links to the conflict over the future role of national versus international IP offices as nations seek to promote so-called innovation cultures;

4 the issue of second-tier protection or even more democratised IP as several interacting forces and interests combine including the needs of small and medium-sized business and the onslaught of the Internet.

US power and the exposed institutional tension in the core IP trade-off

The core trade-off between protection and dissemination is inherent in the existence and roles of IP agencies. To some extent, therefore, there has always been a tension at their institutional core. The book has shown how this tension has been particularly exposed and brought into the political limelight in the 1980s and 1990s to a greater extent than before. In short, IP has simply become more politicised in recent years, largely through the exercise of US economic and political power. It has also been influenced by a wider set of debates and interests within and outside the state. It has brought the IP agencies out of their prior state of contented operational and technically centred obscurity.

This change is due to several interwoven developments in the enhanced place of IP policy in national and international economic policy priorities:

- the decline of traditional industrial policy and hence of the previously preferred instruments of protection, the tariff and subsidies;
- the ascendancy of trade-related competitiveness strategies and policies for a knowledge-based economy and hence the search for new instruments of protection, including some aspects of IP;
- the subtle but quite vital fact that IP is but one part of a more seamless web of public and private actions needed to yield innovation in the modern knowledge economy.

The closely connected political reality which emerges is that copyright policy has become more politically and institutionally integrated within IP institutions largely because of the aggressive unilateralism of US trade politics and strategy. We have shown how this was linked to changes in the IP and trade policy machinery of the US Government and how these changes have reached out to affect international IP bodies such as WIPO by giving prominence to the WTO and its dispute-settlement disciplines.

For the foreseeable future, it is US aggressiveness, more than any other factor, that is driving IP policy and institutional change. This is because the USA has an industrial policy and it is manifest in using trade regimes that are more and more centred in the protections and advantages that can be secured through intellectual property rights. Within the US political system, it is major IP firms and sectors that are leading and mobilising on the trade policy front, to consolidate the US gains made in the TRIPs agreement and elsewhere in the world trade policy agenda.

The discussion of copyright institutions and the WTO–TRIPs system especially reinforces this picture of US aggressiveness, particularly on the insistence that WTO dispute-settlement processes underpin the new international compliance and enforcement system. We have shown, however, that US views face a challenge or an alternative paradigm, especially in the copyright realm where European linkages of copyright to cultural policy are important and persistent.

The exposure of the tension in the core IP trade-off is also a function of the IP agencies' transformation into reinvented executive or operating agency status. The central reason for this is that the reinvented government ethos essentially seeks to ensure that agencies become more conscious of precisely who their clients and customers are. It seeks to break up the standard relationships that have dominated the more traditional bureaucratic modes of operation. Because of agency status, but also because of a generally greater government-wide awareness of a service ethic, all the agencies are attempting to give more overt recognition to the broader IP dissemination roles. This means a broadening sense of their own clients and of the interests with which they must develop close working relations. This development is basically positive simply on the grounds that there is a better awareness of the actual needs of a more diverse clientele. But it is not without its severe growing pains, a point to which we return in the later discussion of national and international office competition. Moreover, the reinvented government model has had a more sluggish development in international agencies, largely because they are still seen as being composed of governments and it is widely believed that they serve governments more than their private sector user communities.

The flexibilities inherent in such forms have been beneficial but have been shown to be greater on the financial side of operations than on the personnel side. No IP agency has complete freedom on its fee-setting functions. Moreover, as we saw in Chapter 3 these reforms do not fundamentally overturn the core features of the national IP agency. The examination of the governing structures of national IP offices indicates that there is a simple but basic need to link the older crucial concept of the 'statutory person' model of regulatory organisation to more recent common changes to establish patent agencies as executive agencies. There are some potential conflicts between these two features of governance in part because the statutory person aspect has a very firm legal basis whereas the executive agency functions are derived from much broader and often non-statutory managerial and, recently, government-wide service delivery mandates. The book has also shown the varied ways in which the policy function has been managed between the operational agencies and the parent policy department, especially industry departments. Industry departments do not necessarily stay out of the business of the IP agencies. Indeed, they appear more and more interested in what they do or at least in how they can be positioned as a part of larger innovation strategies.

The continuing dominance of the protection role: pendency, efficiency and big business

A second overall conclusion is that, despite the exposed tension in the core IP trade-off, the main mandate and institutional culture of the IP agencies are still overwhelmingly centred on the protection role. The main IP agencies still essentially revolve around the core business or case application and operational cycles. This is the bread and butter of their existence and defines their organisational and regulatory cultures. Differences between purely national versus international agency mandates must, of course, be recognised but in the EPO and the WIPO the protection mandate is also at the heart of their operations and of their financial viability.

Beyond this central fact, the actual mandates and missions of the particular IP agencies reveal some differences in emphasis. Differences range from the partial constitutional status of US IP rights to the specific ways in which the agencies have embraced the credo of commercially oriented, independent and client-oriented 'reinvented' agencies.

Big business concerns about basic pendency performance and the efficiency and quality of the patent or trademark application process reinforces the protection function even more. The analysis has shown that there has been increased pressure, led by large IP firms and industrial interest groups, to improve and make more transparent the performance criteria of such examination and registration operations. This, in turn, is crucially tied to agency fees and hence agency financial viability as all agencies become executive or special corporate bodies with greater financial freedoms. Big business pressures have also been the main impetus to change the length and quality of IP protection. The TRIPs negotiations saw the realisation of a harmonised 20-year rule despite other analytical logic which suggests that time periods could vary by sector or between developing and developed countries.

The protection function has also been significantly influenced by international concerns about enforcement, especially in the copyright realm of IP but in other realms as well. The analysis has shown further ways in which this has influenced and forced new arrangements between WIPO and the WTO and with the formation of the TRIPs Council. After some initial tensions there seems little doubt that both WIPO and WTO will have much to do in the now shared space they occupy in the IP institutional terrain.

The analysis of trademarks and copyright and the more detailed look at the WTO–TRIPs only reinforces the conclusions about the dominance of the protection function. In trademarks, the IP agencies are also under pressure to improve pendency performance, in part because trademarks in some jurisdictions are growing at a faster rate than patents. In copyright regimes as a whole, there is also little doubt that the rights of authors/creators are being strengthened relative to those interests which advocate fair or free use of their creations.

Financial interdependence, agency competition and the issue of who should play, and pay for the new dissemination roles

A third concluding issue centres around the IP dissemination roles and the issues related to who should carry them out and who should pay for them. There is, at one level, a desirable tendency for IP agencies to try to increase awareness of IP, especially among small and medium-sized enterprises. But given the multi-faceted links between such activities and other aspects of promoting innovation, it is not clear that IP agencies on their own can do the job or, indeed, will be allowed to do it. Industry departments have some advantages in this regard but they often lack IP expertise.

There is inevitably a connection between who can and should pay for the larger IP dissemination roles and thus the issue of the financial interdependence of the agencies comes into play. The logic of a totally fee-dependent 'executive agency' IP body suggests that fees come from those who already use the IP system and obtain protection. If the larger dissemination role is a public goods or public interest role then there is a justifiable call on tax resources. But with tax resources come controls that are not necessarily compatible with the broad thrust of the executive or special operating agency model.

The analysis suggests that the IP professions are extremely reluctant and sceptical of the effort to shift more attention to the IP dissemination role and, by implication therefore, away from the protection function. The interests of the IP profession are not identical with big business but it is important nonetheless to identify both the differences and the similarities in their positions as the dominant interests in the protection role. They both bring to the IP agencies, especially under the conditions of globalisation, a strong pressure to improve the efficiency of pendency but also its quality. IP agencies themselves are increasingly seeking to broaden their own sense of their clientele beyond these two primary sets of interests, but, at the same time, they know that they are extremely dependent on big business and the profession.

The analysis of trademark institutions shows in one sense that dissemination in this IP realm has a much more subdued meaning than in the realm of patents. This is because trademarks are embedded in subtle aspects of marketing, firm and product identity and commercial selling. Trademarks therefore contain less of a stock of knowledge that others can use to advance innovation except very indirectly.

The addition of the copyright regime raises more stark issues because dissemination involves the debate between commercial permission to copy and thus distribute or publish, and concepts of fair use. Fair use realms seem to be receding, however, precisely on the grounds that those institutions (education institutions, broadcasters etc.) who had the use of others' creations for free, or close to free, should now have to pay. Dissemination in copyright does have another element as well, namely the perceived greater need for programmes of education to promote awareness of copyright as a moral and economic right.

These points are all ultimately linked to the broad nature of overall relations between national and international IP agencies. There is without doubt a good level of cooperation among national and international bodies but there is also a growing sense of considerable competition as well. As harmonisation pressures increase and with protection roles 'moving up' to regional IP bodies there is likely to be increased concern about just what the national IP agencies will and should do.

A logical division of labour could be that smaller national bodies would focus on dissemination roles directed at their small and medium-sized businesses. But it is not clear that an agency or ministry has the right kinds of expertise for this bifurcated activity without having the protection role itself. Moreover, crucial issues arise as to how this is financed if fees (from the protection function) are gone or seriously reduced. Moreover, national IP professions will likely resist such developments and, more generally, national governments may support their national offices on nationalistic grounds or because crucial language issues are involved.

One final cautionary point, inherently a common sense one, is that with respect to overall structure, there is an obvious need to both appreciate and respect the different dynamics of international bodies, such as WIPO and EPO, compared to national agencies. It is simply a fact of life that because it is nation states which are the members of the governing bodies of WIPO and the EPO, their decision processes have been and are necessarily slower and consensual. The differences between WIPO and EPO have also been shown, particularly regarding the fact that the representatives on the EPO are typically the heads of national patent offices in Europe. Many such offices have a strong sensitivity to the competitive needs of their own institutions. But the EPO also contains nation states which do not have IP agencies or which have only limited registration-type agencies. As for the practice and politics of language it is crucial to stress that this does not matter only to governments but also to businesses, especially small and medium-sized businesses.

When trademarks are added to the analytical picture a further variable is present. It suggests that national offices, as they search for viable roles, may pay more attention to their trademark mandates in part because they involve functions and clientele that are more national/local and hence viable as a part of the longer term institutional survival of national offices.

Two-tiered protection and the potential for more 'democratised' IP institutions

Without doubt, the most speculative area that emerges for final commentary is the broader issue of two-tiered protection and the related aspects of IP governance and democracy suggested by the Internet and related aspects of technological change. The book has shown that, perhaps partly because of the big business pressures mentioned earlier, counterpressures are emerging more strongly from small and medium-sized businesses and small inventor groups for alternate utility models or petty patents. They have often argued for shorter, less expensive, and less rigorous forms of protection.

We have also suggested, much more speculatively, that competition laws and IP laws and regimes may collide in the coming years because of somewhat related divisions in the business community within and among nations. This prospect is especially likely if IP is seen to become internationally the protectionist 'weapon of choice', replacing the tariff and subsidies for the world's most powerful firms and nations. Biotechnology inventions and environmental framework laws may also collide more frequently or will at least need a considerable sorting out.

The metaphorical notion of 'second-tier' protection or weaker looser protection might however be something to retain as a concept regarding the Internet. This is because the democratisation or participative nature of the Internet may indeed be gradually yielding, in the trademark and copyright fields especially, a set of interests and pressures that will push for a much looser regime of rules. The domain names issue examined in Chapter 6 and the debate about the information highway do not show this definitively but there are interests now in play that may change things considerably. No definitive final view of these impacts is possible here although the instinct of the author is that they are likely to produce major institutional change rather than mere adaptation at the margin. This is because the array of interests being formed in and around the information highway and the Internet is extremely broad and is likely to change IP politics and eventually institutions in a major way.

These emerging conflicts are not simply a function of how to manage it in a narrow sense but also because the Internet brings into play an array of players, indeed 'networks of networks' of interests, who are much more likely than existing IP bodies to see the need for processes that are less rule ridden and bureaucratic.

An understanding of the core trade-off inherent in intellectual property will become more and more crucial as a new century dawns. There is little doubt that efforts to globalise property have been the dominant trend in the last decade but an examination of IP agencies suggests that counterforces may emerge to reconfigure the trade-off once again.

Bibliography

'A Conference on Intellectual Property Rights and the Arts – the Impact of New Technology' (1996) in *Leonardo*, **29** (3).

Abbott, Frederick M. (1989) 'Protecting First World Assets in the Third World: Intellectual Property Negotiations in the GATT Multilateral Framework', *Vanderbilt Journal of Transnational Law*, **22** (4), pp. 689–746.

Acharya, R. (1992) 'Patenting of Biotechnology: GATT and the Erosion of the World's Biodiversity', *Journal of World Trade*, **25** (6), pp. 71–87.

Advisory Council on Industrial Property (1995) *Review of the Petty Patent System* (Canberra: Australian Industrial Property Organization).

American Intellectual Property Law Association (1995) *Statement to the Subcommittee on Courts and Intellectual Property, Committee on the Judiciary, House of Representatives*. Statement on Bills to Incorporate the Patent and Trademark Office, Washington, September, 14.

Anderman, Steve (1998) *EC Competition Law and Intellectual Property Rights* (Oxford: Oxford University Press).

Anderson, S.S. and Kjell Eliassen (eds) (1993) *Making Policy in Europe* (London: Sage).

Aoki, K. (1996) '(Intellectual) Property and Sovereignty – Notes Towards a Cultural Geography of Authorship', *Stanford Law Review*, **48** (5), pp. 1293–1355.

Archer, Clive (1992) *International Organizations* 2nd edn (London: Routledge).

Ashford, Tony (1996) 'Regulating Agricultural Biotechnology: Reflexive Modernization and the European Union', *Policy and Politics*, **24** (2) (April), pp. 125–136.

Assistant Secretary of Commerce and Commissioner of Patents and Trademarks (1993) *Annual Report: Fiscal Year 1993* (Washington: US Department of Commerce).

Aucoin, Peter (1997) *The New Public Management: Canada in Comparative Perspective* (Montreal: McGill-Queens University Press).

Australia (1996) *Review of the Regulatory Regime for Patent Attorneys* (Canberra: Minister for Science and Technology).

Australian Industrial Property Organization (AIPO) (1994) *Strategic Directions 1994–98* (Canberra: AIPO).

Australian Industrial Property Organization (1994a) *Activities Report 1993–94* (Canberra: AIPO).

Australian Industrial Property Organization (1995) *Strategic Directions 1995–99* (Canberra: AIPO).

Bainbridge, David I. (1994) *Intellectual Property* 2nd edn (London: Pitman).

Baldwin, John (1997) *Innovation and Intellectual Property* (Ottawa: Statistics Canada and Industry Canada).

Barlow, John Perry (1994) 'The Economy of Ideas: A Framework for Rethinking Patents and Copyrights in the Digital Age (Everything You Know About Intellectual Property is Wrong)', *Wired*, March, pp. 84–89.

Beier, Friedrich-Karl and G. Schricker (1989) 'GATT or WIPO? New Ways in the International Protection of Intellectual Property', *Studies in Industrial Property and Copyright Law* (Weinheim).

Bellamy, Christine and John A. Taylor (1998) *Governing in the Information Age* (Buckingham: Open University Press).

Bennett, A. LeRoy (1995) *International Organizations: Principles and Issues* 6th edn (Englewood Cliffs, NJ: Prentice Hall).

Best, Michael (1990) *The New Competition: Institutions of Industrial Restructuring* (Cambridge: Polity Press).

Bhagwati, J. and H.T. Patrick (eds) (1990) *Aggressive Unilateralism* (Ann Arbor: Michigan University Press).

Bhat, M.G. (1996) 'Trade Related Intellectual Property Rights To Biological Research – Socioeconomic Implications for Developing Countries', *Ecological Economics*, **19** (3), pp. 205–217.

Bogsch, Arpad (1992) *Brief History of the First 25 Years of the World Intellectual Property Organization* (Geneva: World Intellectual Property Organization).

Bradley, Jane (1987) 'Intellectual Property Rights, Investment, and Trade in Services in the Uruguay Round: Laying the Foundations', *Stanford Journal of International Law*, Spring, pp. 57–98.

Braga, Carlos Prima (1995) 'Trade Related Intellectual Property Issues: The Uruguay Round Agreement and its Economic Implications', in Will Martin and Alan Winters (eds) *The Uruguay Round and the Developing Countries* (Washington: World Bank).

Braunstein, Y.M. (1995) 'Fair Use, Intellectual Property and Universal Service in an Interactive, Networked Society', *Canadian Journal of Information and Library Science*, **20** (3 and 4), pp. 34–40.

Brown, Kenneth (1988) *Inventors at Work* (Washington: Tempus Books).

Brunet, C. (1994) *Copyright and the Information Highway* Draft Final Report of the Copyright Subcommittee, September.

Burk, Dan L. (1994) 'Transborder Intellectual Property Issues on the Electronic Frontier', *Stanford Law and Policy Review*, **9**, pp. 221–240.

Buxton, Tony, Paul Chapman and Paul Temple (1997) *Britain's Economic Performance* (London: Routledge).

Campbell, Colin (1996) 'Does Reinvented Government Need Reinvention?', *Governance* **8** (4), pp. 479–504.

Campbell, Robert M. and Leslie A. Pal (1994) *The Real Worlds of Canadian Politics* 3rd edn (Peterborough: Broadview Press).

Canada (1984) *From Gutenberg to Telidon: A White Paper on Copyright* (Ottawa: Minister of Supply and Services).

Canada (1995) *Connection, Community, Content: The Challenge of the Information Highway* (Ottawa: Minister of Supply and Services).

Canada (1997) *Review of the Patent Act Amendment Act 1992* (Ottawa: Industry Canada).

Canadian Intellectual Property Office (1993) *Business Plan 1993–94 to 1995–96* (Ottawa: Canadian Intellectual Property Office).

Canadian Intellectual Property Office (1994) *1992–1993 Annual Report* (Ottawa: Industry Canada).

Canadian Intellectual Property Office (1994a) *CIPO Regional Intermediary Conferences: Final Report* (Ottawa: CIPO).

Canadian Intellectual Property Office (1995) *Business Plan 1995–96 to 1997–98* (Ottawa: Canadian Intellectual Property Office).

Chartered Institute of Patent Agents (1985) *Response to the Office of Fair Trading Enquiry* (London: Chartered Institute of Patent Agents).

Chartered Institute of Patent Agents (1994) *Second Tier Protection* Report and Proceedings of a Symposium on Utility Models, Brocket Hall, Hertfordshire, July 6–8.

Chartrand, H.H. (1996) 'Intellectual Property Rights in the Postmodern World', *Journal of Arts, Management, Law and Society*, **25** (4), pp. 306–319.

Chieruale, E. (1997) 'Asserting US Intellectual Property Rights in China: Expansion of Extraterritorial Jurisdiction', *Journal of Copyright System of USA*, **44** (3), pp. 198–230.

Church, Jeffrey and Roger Ware (1997) 'Trade-dress and Pharmaceuticals: Efficiency, Competition and Intellectual Property Rights', *Policy Options*, **18** (8), pp. 13–16.

Clark, Aubert J. (1960) *The Movement For International Copyright in Nineteenth Century America* (New York: Free Press).

Coates, David (ed.) (1996) *Industrial Policy in Britain* (London: Macmillan).

Commission of the European Communities (1995) *Green Paper: Copyright and Related Rights in the Information Economy* (Brussels, Commission of the European Communities).

Commission of the European Communities (1995a) *Green Paper: Protection of Utility Models in the Single Market* (Brussels: Commission of the European Communities).

Consumer and Corporate Affairs Canada (1990) *Intellectual Property and Canada's Commercial Interests* (Ottawa: Minister of Supply and Services).

Cook, T., C. Doyle and D. Jabbari (1991) *Pharmaceuticals, Biotechnology and the Law* (London: Macmillan).

Coombe, Rosemary J. (1994) 'Challenging Paternity: Histories of Copyright', *Yale Journal of Law and Humanities* (book review), **6**, pp. 397–399.

Copyright Board Canada (1991) Internal Document. Presentation made by Vice President on Functions of the Copyright Board, December.

Copyright Board Canada (1996) *Annual Report 1995–1996*. Ottawa.

Copyright Board Canada (1996a) Submission of the Copyright Board on Bill C-32, An Act to Amend the Copyright Act, to the Standing Committee on Canadian Heritage, September 3.

Cornish, W.R. (1996) *Intellectual Property* 3rd edn (London: Sweet and Maxwell).

Crandall, R.W. and I. Waverman (1995) *Talk is Cheap: The Promise of Regulatory Reform in North American Telecommunications* (Washington: The Brookings Institution).

Curtis, John (1990) 'Intellectual Property and International Trade', *Institute of Development Studies Bulletin*, University of Sussex, **21**, January.

Davis, G. (1994) *Copyright and the Public Interest* (IIC Studies, vol. 14) (Weinheim: VCH Verlagsgesellschaft mbH).

de la Mothe, John and Gilles Paquet (1996) *Evolutionary Economics and the New International Political Economy* (London: Pinter).

Department of Industry, Science and Technology (1995) *Australian Industrial Property Organization: Activities Report 1994–95* (Canberra: Commonwealth of Australia).

Department of Justice, Industry Canada and Canadian Heritage (1995) *Symposium on Digital Technology and Copyright* (Ottawa: Minister of Public Works and Government Services Canada).

Dewees, Donald N. (ed.) (1983) *The Regulation of Quality* (Toronto: Butterworths).

Diebold, John (1990) *The Innovators* (New York: Truman Talley Books).

Doern, G. Bruce (1987) *Modernizing Economic Framework Legislation: A Discussion Paper* (Ottawa: Consumer and Corporate Affairs Canada).

Doern, G. Bruce (1994) *The Road To Better Public Services: Progress and Constraints in Five Federal Agenices* (Montreal: C.D. Howe Institute).

Doern, G. Bruce (1995) *The Regulation of Patent and Trade-Mark Agent Qualifications: Institutional Issues and Options* (Ottawa: Canadian Intellectual Property Office).

Doern, G. Bruce (1995a) 'A Political-Institutional Framework For the Analysis of Competition Policy Institutions', *Governance*, April, pp. 195–217.

Doern, G. Bruce (1995b) *Fairer Play: Canadian Competition Policy Institutions in a Global Market* (Toronto: C.D. Howe Institute).

Doern, G. Bruce (1995c) 'The Formation of Industry Canada: Second Beginnings For a Department of The Micro-Economy', Paper presented to the Workshop on the 1993 Federal Reorganization, Canadian Centre for Management Development.

Doern, G. Bruce (1996) 'Looking for the Core: Industry Canada and Program Review', in Gene Swimmer (ed.) *How Ottawa Spends: 1996–97: Life Under the Knife* (Ottawa: Carleton University Press).

Doern, G. Bruce (1997) 'The European Patent Office and the Political Economy of European Intellectual Property Policy', *Journal of European Public Policy*, **4** (3).

Doern, G. Bruce and Brian W. Tomlin (1991) *Faith and Fear: The Free Trade Story* (Toronto: Stoddart).

Doern, G. Bruce and Stephen Wilks (eds) (1996) *National Competition Policy Institutions in a Global Market* (Oxford: Clarendon Press).

Doern, G. Bruce and Stephen Wilks (eds) (1998) *Changing Regulatory Institutions in Britain and North America* (Toronto: University of Toronto Press).

Doern, G. Bruce, Leslie Pal and Brian Tomlin (eds) (1996) *Crossing Borders: The Internationalization of Canadian Public Policy* (Toronto: Oxford University Press).

Doremus, P.N. (1996) 'The Externalization of Domestic Regulation – Intellectual Property Rights Reform in a Global Era', *Science Communication*, **17** (2), pp. 137–162.

Drahos, P. (1996) 'Global Law Reform and Rent-Seeking: The Case of Intellectual Property', *Australian Journal of Corporate Law*, **7**, pp. 45–61.

Drahos, P. (1997) 'Thinking Strategically about Intellectual Property Rights', *Telecommunications Policy*, **21** (3), pp. 201–11.

Drake, W.J. (1994) 'Asymmetric Deregulation and the Transformation of the International Telecommunications Regime' in E. Noam and G. Pogorel (eds) *Asymmetric Deregulation: The Dynamics of Telecommunications Policy in Europe and the United States* (Norwood, NJ: Ablex Publishing).

Drake, W.J. (ed.) (1995) *The New Information Infrastructure: Strategies For US Policy* (New York: Twentieth Century Fund Press).

Drake, William and Kalypso Nicolaidis (1992) 'Ideas, Interests and Institutionalization: "Trade in Services" and the Uruguay Round', *International Organization*, **46** (4), pp. 37–100.

Eastman, Harry (1985) *Report of the Commission of Inquiry on the Pharmaceutical Industry* (Ottawa: Minister of Supply and Services).

Economic Council of Canada (1971) *Report on Intellectual and Industrial Property* (Ottawa: Information Canada).

Edquist, Charles (ed.) (1997) *Systems of Innovation: Technologies, Institutions and Organizations* (London: Pinter).

Elkins, David J. (1995) *Beyond Sovereignty; Territory and Political Economy in the Twenty-First Century* (Toronto: University of Toronto Press).

European Patent Office (1992) *The European Patent Office* (Munich: European Patent Office).

European Patent Office (1992a) *How To Get a European Patent* (Munich: European Patent Office).

European Patent Office (1994) *National Law Relating To The EPO* (Munich: European Patent Office).

European Patent Office (1994a) *Utilization of Patent Protection in Europe*. Published as Volume 3 of *EPOScript* (Munich: European Patent Office).

European Patent Office (1995) *European Patent Office: Annual Report 1994* (Munich: European Patent Office).

Fédération Internationale des Conseils en Propriété Industrielle (FICPI) (1992) *Revue et Bulletin*, Congrès Mondiale, 1988 (London: FICPI).

Fédération Internationale des Conseils en Propriété Industrielle (1993) 'The Worldwide Association of Intellectual Property' Brochure.

Feketekuty, Geza (1991) 'Intellectual Property – The Major Shifts that are Taking Place in the World Economy', in Murray G. Smith (ed.) *Global Rivalry and Intellectual Property* (Montreal: Institute For Research on Public Policy).

Ferlie, Ewan, Lynn Ashburner, Louise Fitzgerald and Andrew Pettigrew (1996) *The New Public Management in Action* (Oxford: Oxford University Press).

Flatow, Ira (1992) *They All Laughed ... From Light Bulbs to Lasers* (New York: HarperCollins).

Frischtak, C.R. (1995) 'Harmonization versus Differentiation in International Property Rights Regimes', *International Journal of Technology Management*, **10** (2–3), pp. 200–213.

Gallini, Nancy T. and Michael Trebilcock (1996) 'Intellectual Property Rights and Competition Policy: An Overview of Legal and Economic Issues' Paper presented to the Symposium on Competition Policy, Intellectual Property Rights and International Economic Integration. Ottawa, May 12–13.

Getlan, M. (1995) 'TRIPS and the Future of Section 301: A Comparative Study in Trade Dispute Resolution', *Columbia Journal of Transnational Law*, **34** (173), pp. 178–184.

Goldstein, Paul (1994) 'Copyright and Author's Right in the Twenty-First Century', *WIPO Worldwide Symposium on the Future of Copyright and Neighboring Rights* (Geneva: WIPO).

Greenwood, Justin and Mark Aspinwall (eds) (1998) *Collective Action in the European Union* (London: Routledge).

Greenwood, J. and K. Konit (1992) 'Established and Emergent Sectors: Organized Interests at the European Level of the Pharmaceutical Industry and the New Biotechnologies', in J. Greenwood, J. Grote and K. Konit (eds) *Organized Interests in the European Community* (London: Sage), pp. 69–98.

Gross, Neil (1995) 'A US Patent Corporation?', *Business Week*, October 30, pp. 76B-E–76D-E.

Gyertyanfy, Peter (1994) 'Using Computer Technology to Solve the Copyright Problems Raised by Computer Technology', *WIPO Worldwide Symposium on the Future of Copyright and Neighboring Rights* (Geneva: WIPO).

Hattenbach, Ben (1995) 'GATT TRIPS and the Small American Inventor: An Evaluation of the Effort to Preserve Domestic Technological Innovation', *Intellectual Property Journal*, **10** (1), pp. 61–98.

Hébert, Monique (1996) Background Paper, Copyright Reform. (Ottawa: Library of Parliament).

Hébert, Monique (1997) *Legislative Summary Bill C-32: An Act to Amend the Copyright Act* (Ottawa: Library of Parliament).

Helpman, E. (1993) 'Innovation, Imitation and Intellectual Property Rights', *Ecomonetrica*, **61** (6), pp. 1247–1280.

Hoekman, Bernard and M. Kostecki (1995) *The Political Economy of The World Trading System: From GATT to WTO* (Oxford: Oxford University Press).

Hogwood, Brian W. (1984) 'The Rise and Fall of the Department of Industry' Paper presented to the Conference of the Structure and Organization of Government Group, International Political Science Association, Manchester, November.

Howitt, Peter (1996) 'On Some Problems of Measuring Knowledge-Based Growth', in Peter Howitt (ed.) *The Implications of Knowledge-Based Growth for Micro-Economic Policies* (Calgary: University of Calgary Press).

Intellectual Property Owners (1995) *Statement Before the Subcommittee on Courts and Intellectual Property, Committee on the Judiciary, House of Representatives.* Statement on Bills to Incorporate the Patent and Trademark Office, Washington, September 14.

International Ad Hoc Committee (1997) *The International Ad Hoc Committee.* http://www.iahc.org/iahc-discuss.

International Trademark Association (1997) *About the International Trademark Association* (New York: INTA).

Jacob, Robin and Daniel Alexander (1993) *A Guidebook to Intellectual Property* 4th edn (London: Sweet and Maxwell).

Jacobson, Harold K. (1984) *Networks of Interdependence: International Organizations and the Global Political System* 2nd edn (London: McGraw-Hill).

Jasanoff, Sheila (1998) *Comparative Science and Technology Policy* (London: Elgar).

Jaszi, Peter (1992) 'On the Author Effect: Contemporary Copyright and Collective Creativity', *Cardozo Arts and Entertainment Law Journal*, **10**, pp. 293–320.

Jussawalla, Meheroo (1992) *The Economics of Intellectual Property in a World Without Frontiers: A Study of Computer Software* (New York: Greenwood).

Keplinger, Michael S. (1995) 'An American View on TRIPs: The Copyright Aspects of the US Implementation Act' Paper presented to the 10th Annual Seminar of the Dutch Foundation for Copyright Protection, Amsterdam, November 10.

Knight, Jackson (1995) *Patent Strategy For Researchers and Research Managers* (London: John Wiley & Sons).

Kratochwil, F. and E. Mansfield (eds) (1994) *International Organization* (New York: HarperCollins).

Kreher, Alexander and Yves Meny (1997) 'European Agencies' Special section of *Journal of European Public Policy*, **4** (2).

Krugman, Paul (1994) 'Competitiveness: A Dangerous Obsession', *Foreign Affairs*, March/April, pp. 28–44.

Levy, Brian and Pablo T. Spiller (eds) (1996) *Regulations, Institutions, and Commitment* (Cambridge: Cambridge University Press).

Lexchin, Joel (1992) *Pharmaceuticals, Patents and Politics: Canada and Bill C-22* (Ottawa: Canadian Centre for Policy Alternatives).

McCormick, John (1996) *The European Union: Politics and Policies* (Boulder, CL: Westview Press).

McFetridge, Donald G. (1996) 'Intellectual Property, Technology Diffusion and Growth' Paper prepared for Symposium on Competition Policy, Intellectual Property Rights and International Economic Integration. Ottawa, May 12–13.

Maher, Imelda (1998) 'Competition Law and Intellectual Property Rights: Evolving Formalism' in Paul Craig and Grainne de Burca (eds) *The Evolution of European Community Law* (Oxford: Oxford University Press).

Majone, G. (1996) Regulating Europe (London: Routledge).

Mango, Anthony (1988) 'The Role of the Secretariats of International Institutions', in Paul Taylor and A.J.R. Groom (eds) *International Institutions at Work* (London: Pinter).

Mansfield, Edwin (1986) 'Patents and Innovation: An Empirical Study', *Management Science*, pp. 173–181.

March, J.G. (1996) 'Institutional Perspectives on Political Institutions', *Governance*, **9** (3), pp. 247–264.

March, J.G. and J.P. Olsen (1989) *Rediscovering Institutions* (New York: Basic Books).

Marlin Bennett, R. (1995) 'International Intellectual Property Rights in a Web of Social Relations', *Science Communication*, **17** (2), pp. 119–136.

Maskus, Keith E. (1991) 'Economic Analysis of Intellectual Property Rights: Domestic and International Dimensions', in Murray G. Smith (ed.) *Global Rivalry and Intellectual Property* (Montreal: Institute For Research on Public Policy).

Maskus, Keith E. (1995) 'Intellectual Property Rights in the Global Information Economy' Paper presented to Conference on Policy Frameworks For A Knowledge Economy, John Deutsch Institute, Queens University, Kingston, November 16–17, 1995.

Merges, Robert (1990) 'Battle of the Lateralisms: Intellectual Property and Trade', *Boston University International Law Journal*, Fall, pp. 239–246.

National Academy of Public Administration (1995) *Statement of Harold Seidman Before the Subcommittee on Courts and Intellectual Property, Committee on the Judiciary, House of Representatives*. A Statement on Bills to Incorporate the Patent and Trademark Office, Washington, September 14.

Nelson, Richard R. (ed.) (1993) *National Innovation Systems: A Comparative Analysis* (Oxford: Oxford University Press).

Niosi, Jorge (1995) *Flexible Innovation: Technological Alliances in Canadian Industry* (Montreal: McGill-Queens University Press).

Office For Harmonization In The Internal Market (1995) *Trade Marks and Designs* (Luxembourg: Office of Official Publications of the European Communities).

Office of Fair Trading (1986) *Review of Restrictions on the Patent Agents Profession* (London: Office of Fair Trading).

Ogus, Anthony (1994) *Regulation: Legal Form and Economic Theory* (Oxford: Clarendon Press).

Okimoto, D. (1989) *Between MITI and the Market* (Stanford: Stanford University Press).

Organization for Economic Cooperation and Development (1989) *Competition Policy and Intellectual Property Rights* (Paris: OECD).

Ostrom, E. (1990) 'Rational Choice Theory and Institutional Analysis: Toward Complementarity', *American Political Science Review*, **85**, pp. 237–243.

Ostry, Sylvia (1990) *Governments and Corporations in a Shrinking World: Trade and Innovation Policies in the United States, Europe and Japan* (New York: Council on Foreign Relations).

Ostry, Sylvia (1991) 'The Place of Intellectual Property Rights in the Evolution of Innovation Policy', in Murray G. Smith (ed.) *Global Rivalry and Intellectual Property* (Montreal: Institute For Research on Public Policy).

Ostry, Sylvia (1993) 'Globalization, Domestic Policies and the Need For Harmonization' Paper presented to Workshop on Competition Policy in a Global Economy, University of California, January 8–9, 1993.

Pal, Leslie A. and Robert M. Campbell (1994) *The Real Worlds of Canadian Politics* 3rd edn (Peterborough: Broadview Press).

Paquet, Gilles and Jeff Roy (1995) 'Prosperity Through Networks: The Bottom-Up Strategy That Might Have Been', in S. Phillips (ed.) *How Ottawa Spends: 1995–96* (Ottawa: Carleton University Press).

Park, W.G. and J.C. Ginarte (1997) 'Intellectual Property Rights and Economic Growth', *Contemporary Economic Policy*, **15** (3), pp. 51–61.

Parrot, François (1994) 'New Technologies and the Protection and Administration of the Rights of Performers', *WIPO Worldwide Symposium on the Future of Copyright and Neighboring Rights* (Geneva: WIPO).

Patel, S.J. (1993) 'Intellectual Property Rights and National Development', *Scientific and Industrial Research*, **52** (4), pp. 220–239.

Patented Medicine Prices Review Board (1995) *Seventh Annual Report* (Ottawa: Patented Medicine Prices Review Board).

Petersman, E.U. and G. Marceau (1997) 'The GATT/WTO Dispute Settlement System – International Law, International Organization and Dispute Settlement', *Journal of World Trade* **31** (3), pp. 169–179.

Petrosky, Henry (1993) *The Evolution of Useful Things* (New York: Knopf).

Phillips, Jeremy and Alison Firth (1995) *Introduction to Intellectual Property Law* 3rd edn (London: Butterworths).

Pollack, Mark A. (1996) 'The New Institutionalism and EC Governance: The Promise and Limits of Institutional Analysis', *Governance*, **9** (4), pp. 429–458.

Porter, Michael (1990) *The Competitive Advantage of Nations* (New York: Free Press).

Prime Minister's Science and Engineering Council (1994) *The Role of Intellectual Property in Innovation* (Canberra: Commonwealth of Australia).

Purdue, Derrick (1995) 'Hegemonic Trips: World Trade, Intellectual Property and Biodiversity', *Environmental Politics*, **4** (1), pp. 88–107.

Rapp, R. and R. Rozak (1990) 'Benefits and Costs of Intellectual Property Protection in Developing Countries', *Journal of World Trade*, **24**, pp. 75–102.

Raymond, C. (1996) *The Economic Importance of Patents* (London: The Intellectual Property Institute).

Reichman, J.H. (1989) 'Intellectual Property in International Trade: Opportunies and Risks of a GATT Connection', *Vanderbilt Journal of Transnational Law*, **22** (4), pp. 747–892.

Renko, Robert P. (1987) *Protecting Intellectual Property Rights: Issues and Controversies* (Washington: University Press of America).

Richetson, S. (1995) 'The Future of the Traditional Intellectual Property Conventions in the Brave New World of Trade-Related Intellectual Property Rights', *IIC-International Rights of Industrial Property and Copyright Law*, **26** (6), pp. 872–899.

Rose, Mark (1993) *Authors and Owners: The Invention of Copyright* (Cambridge: Harvard University Press).

Rosenberg, Nathan and Richard Nelson (1994) 'American Universities and Technical Advance in Industry', *Research Policy*, **23** (2), pp. 127–136.

Roy, J. (1995) 'Understanding Governance in High-Technology Regions: Towards a New Paradigm of High Technology and Local Development in Canada' (Ottawa: School of Public Administration, Carleton University).

Samuelson, Pamela (1995) 'Adapting Copyright to Meet the Challenges Posed By Digital Technologies', in Department of Justice, Industry Canada and Canadian Heritage, *Symposium on Digital Technology and Copyright* (Ottawa: Minister of Public Works and Government Services Canada).

Searing, D.D. (1991) 'Roles, Rules and Rationality in the New Institutionalism', *American Political Science Review*, **85**, pp. 1239–1260.

Sell, Susan K. (1995) 'Intellectual Property Protection and Antitrust in the Developing World: Crisis, Coercion and Choice', *International Organization*, **49** (2), pp. 315–349.

Sherman, Brad (1995) 'Remembering and Forgetting: The Birth of Modern Copyright Law', *Intellectual Property Journal*, **10** (1), pp. 1–34.

Sherwood, Robert (1990) *Intellectual Property and Economic Development* (Boulder, CL: Westview Press).

Siebeck, Wolfgang (ed.) (1990) *Strengthening Protection of Intellectual Property in Developing Countries* (Washington: World Bank).

Sirinelli, Pierre (1994) 'The Adaptation of Copyright in the Face of New Technology', *WIPO Worldwide Symposium on the Future of Copyright and Neighboring Rights* (Geneva: WIPO).

Smith, Douglas A. (1984) *Collective Agencies for the Administration of Copyright* (Ottawa: Supply and Services Canada).

Smith, Douglas A. (1988) 'Recent Proposals For Copyright Revision: An Evaluation', *Canadian Public Policy*, **XIV** (2), pp. 175–185.

Smith, Murray (ed.) (1991) *Global Rivalry and Intellectual Property: Developing Canadian Strategies* (Montreal: Institute for Research on Public Policy).

Subramanian, A. (1990) 'TRIPS and the Paradigm of the GATT: A Tropical and Temperate View', *World Economy*, **13** (4), pp. 509–521.

'Symposium: Toward a Third Intellectual Property Paradigm' (1994) *Columbia Law Review*, **94**.

Taylor, Paul (1993) *International Organization in the Modern World* (London: Pinter).

Taylor, Paul and A.J.R. Groom (eds) (1988) *International Institutions at Work* (London: Pinter).

Thurow, Lester C. (1997) 'Needed: A New System of Intellectual Property Rights', *Harvard Business Review*, **75** (3), pp. 94–103.

Toubon, Jacques (1994) 'Welcoming Address' in World Intellectual Property Organization, *WIPO Worldwide Symposium on the Future of Copyright and Neighboring Rights* (Geneva: WIPO).

Tournier, Jean-Loup (1994) 'The Implications of New Technology for the Protection and Collective Management of Authors' Rights', *WIPO Worldwide Symposium on the Future of Copyright and Neighboring Rights* (Geneva: WIPO).

Trebilcock, Michael and Robert Howse (1995) *The Regulation of International Trade* (London: Routledge).

Tyson, Laura D'Andrea (1993) *Who's Bashing Whom? Trade Conflict in High Technology Industries* (Washington: Institute For International Economics).

US General Accounting Office (1993) *Intellectual Property Rights: US Companies' Patent Experiences in Japan* (Washington; USGAO, GGD-93-126, July).

US Information Infrastructure Task Force (1995) *Intellectual Property and the National Information Infrastructure* (Washington: Department of Commerce).

US Patent and Trademark Office (1993) *Planning Progress Report: Fiscal Years 1994–1998* (Washington: USPTO).

US Patent and Trademark Office (1994) *Strategic Plan 1996–2000* (Washington: USPTO).

US Patent and Trademark Office (1995) *Working For Our Customers: A Patent and Trademark Office Review Fiscal Year 1994* (Washington: USPTO).

US Patent and Trademark Office (1998)*Trademark Examination of Domain Names* (Washington: USPTO).

United Kingdom, Department of Trade and Industry (1995) *Trade and Industry 1995: The Government's Expenditure Plans 1995–96 to 1997–98* (London: HMSO).

United Kingdom Patent Office (1990) *Framework Document 1990* (London: The Patent Office).

United Kingdom Patent Office (1994) *Annual Report* (Newport: The Patent Office).

Vaver, David (1995) 'Rejuvenating Copyright, Digitally', in Department of Justice, Industry Canada, Canadian Heritage, *Symposium on Digital Technology and Copyright* (Ottawa: Minister of Public Works and Government Services Canada).

Wade, Robert (1990) *Governing the Market* (Princeton: Princeton University Press).

Walker, Charles E. and Mark A. Bloomfield (eds) (1988) *Intellectual Property Rights and Capital Formation in the Next Decade* (London: University of America Press).

Wallerstein, M.B., M.E. Mogee and R.A. Schoen (eds) (1993) *Global Dimensions of Intellectual Property Rights in Science and Technology* (Washington: National Academy Press).

Warshovsky, Fred (1994) *The Patent Wars: The Battle to own the World's Technology* (New York: Wiley).

Weiss, Linda (1998) *The Myth of the Powerless State: Governing the Economy in a Global Era* (London: Polity Press).

Westaway, Cynthia (1997) 'Copyright Legislation: Ambushed By the Heritage Committee', *CAUT Bulletin*, **44** (2), pp. 1 and 7.

Wilks, Stephen, Patrick Dunleavy, A. Gamble, Ian Holliday and Gillian Peele (1993) 'Economic Policy' in Patrick Dunleavy *Developments in British Politics* (London: Macmillan).

Woodmansee, Martha and Peter Jaszi (1994) *The Construction of Authorship: Textual Appropriation in Law and Literature*.

World Intellectual Property Organization (1994) *WIPO Worldwide Symposium on the Future of Copyright and Neighboring Rights* (Geneva: World Intellectual Property Organization).

World Intellectual Property Organization (1994a) *Worldwide Forum on the Arbitration of Intellectual Property Disputes* (Geneva: World Intellectual Property Organization).

World Intellectual Property Organization (1995) *Intellectual Property Reading Material* (Geneva: World Intellectual Property Organization).

World Intellectual Property Organization (1995a) *WIPO: General Information* (Geneva: World Intellectual Property Organization).

World Intellectual Property Organization (1995b) *Conference on Rules For Institutional Arbitration and Mediation* (Geneva: World Intellectual Property Organization).

World Intellectual Property Organization (1995c) *Governing Bodies of WIPO and the Unions Administered by WIPO*. Twenty-sixth Series of Meetings, Geneva, September 25 to October 3, pp. 99–102.

World Intellectual Property Organization (1995d) *Governing Bodies of WIPO and the Unions Administered by WIPO*. Twenty-sixth Series of Meetings, Geneva, September 25 to October 3. Draft Program and Budget for the 1996–97 Biennium, p. 19.

World Intellectual Property Organization (1997) *General Information* (Geneva: World Intellectual Property Organization).

World Intellectual Property Organization (1997a) *Consultative Meeting on Trademarks and Internet Domain Names* (Geneva: World Intellectual Property Organization).

World Intellectual Property Organization (1997b) *An Open Letter From The World Intellectual Property Organization (WIPO) to the Internet Community* (Geneva: World Intellectual Property Organization).

World Intellectual Property Organization (1997c) *Chairman's Summary: Consultative Meeting on Trademarks and Internet Domain Names* (Geneva: World Intellectual Property Organization).

World Intellectual Property Organization (1997d) 'Acceptance Speech of the new Director General of WIPO, Dr Kamil Idris', September 22 (Geneva: World Intellectual Property Organization).

World Intellectual Property Organization (1997e) 'Director General Idris Addresses the Staff of WIPO and UPOV', November 20 (Geneva: World Intellectual Property Organization).

World Trade Organization (1996) *Report (1996) of the Council For TRIPS* (Geneva: World Trade Organization).

Wyatt, Geoffrey (1986) *The Economics of Invention* (London: Wheatsheaf).

Yamin, F. (1993) *Intellectual Property Rights and the Environment: The Role of Patents in the Conservation of Biodiversity* LLM Dissertation, Kings College, London.

Yarbrough, Beth and Robert Yarbrough (1990) 'International Institutions and the New Economics of Organization', *International Organization*, **44** (2), pp. 235–259.

Index